T0215323

Introducing Disaster Recovery with Microsoft Azure

Understanding Services and Tools for Implementing a Recovery Solution

Bapi Chakraborty
Yashajeet Chowdhury

Apress®

Introducing Disaster Recovery with Microsoft Azure: Understanding Services and Tools for Implementing a Recovery Solution

Bapi Chakraborty
Bengaluru, Karnataka, India

Yashajeet Chowdhury
Bangalore, Karnataka, India

ISBN-13 (pbk): 978-1-4842-5916-0
https://doi.org/10.1007/978-1-4842-5917-7

ISBN-13 (electronic): 978-1-4842-5917-7

Managing Director, Apress Media LLC: Welmoed Spahr
Acquisitions Editor: Smriti Srivastava
Development Editor: Matthew Moodie
Coordinating Editor: Shrikant Vishwakarma

Cover designed by eStudioCalamar

Cover image designed by Freepik (www.freepik.com)

Distributed to the book trade worldwide by Springer Science+Business Media New York, 233 Spring Street, 6th Floor, New York, NY 10013. Phone 1-800-SPRINGER, fax (201) 348-4505, e-mail orders-ny@springer-sbm.com, or visit www.springeronline.com. Apress Media, LLC is a California LLC and the sole member (owner) is Springer Science + Business Media Finance Inc (SSBM Finance Inc). SSBM Finance Inc is a **Delaware** corporation.

For information on translations, please e-mail rights@apress.com, or visit http://www.apress.com/rights-permissions.

Apress titles may be purchased in bulk for academic, corporate, or promotional use. eBook versions and licenses are also available for most titles. For more information, reference our Print and eBook Bulk Sales web page at http://www.apress.com/bulk-sales.

Any source code or other supplementary material referenced by the author in this book is available to readers on GitHub via the book's product page, located at www.apress.com/978-1-4842-5916-0. For more detailed information, please visit http://www.apress.com/source-code.

Printed on acid-free paper

Table of Contents

About the Authors

Bapi Chakraborty has more than 16 years of IT experience in the field of on-premises and cloud infrastructure architecture, solution design, migration, deployment, and support practices. He has worked with customers and partners from various industries and understands their unique demands and requirements to achieve business goals. He holds various industry and product certification including Microsoft, AWS, and IASA.

Yashajeet Chowdhury has more than 17 years of IT experience in the field of on-premises and cloud infrastructure architecture, solution design, migration, deployment, and support practices. He has deep technical hands-on experience on various infrastructure services including datacenter consolidation and migration, virtualization, cloud computing, and other infrastructure offerings for various small and enterprise customers. He has strong knowledge in architecting, designing, and implementation, and holds many professional technical certifications, including those from Microsoft and IBM.

About the Technical Reviewer

 **Shijimol Ambi Karthikeyan** currently works as a cloud consultant with Microsoft. She has more than 12 years of experience in IT and specializes in datacenter management, virtualization, and cloud computing technologies. She started her career with EY IT services on the datacenter management team managing complex virtualized production datacenters. She has expertise in managing VMware and Hyper-V virtualization stacks and Windows/Linux server technologies. She has also worked on Devops CI/CD implementation projects using tools like TeamCity, Jenkins, Git, TortoiseSVN, Mercurial, Selenium, and more. She later moved into cloud computing and gained expertise in Windows Azure, focusing on Azure IaaS, Backup/DR and Automation. She holds industry standard certifications in technologies including Microsoft Azure, Windows Server, and VMware. She also holds ITIL and TOGAF9 certifications. She has previously authored a book on Azure Automation.

Acknowledgments

I would like to thank my parents for their blessings and support for everything that I have achieved in my life. Their teaching and encouragement always help me to take up new challenges without fear of failure through the journey of life.

My heartful thanks go to my wife Maninder, who is always by my side, supporting my every step. I thank my two divine angels, son Shouvik and daughter Ananya, who always bring new perspectives to life, understanding my unavailability and asking questions that makes me think about how I can explain concepts in a simpler way.

Yashajeet, my coauthor, deserves thanks for bringing this effort together. Most important, he had faith in the idea and extended great collaboration, without which this book would not have seen the light.

Sincere thanks go to the Apress team for their support, guidance, and assistance during the entire publication process.

—Bapi Chakraborty

I want to take the opportunity to thank my parents for all their blessings and support. Their teaching and encouragement has always helped me to grow, keep a positive outlook about life, and be fearless about failure in any situation. Their lessons gave me the strength to face any challenges in life. The most significant thing they have given me is the perspective to look at life and the challenges and take affirmative action toward them.

I would like to take a moment to aacknowledge two people in my life, Natasha and my angel daughter Aadhya, who are my inspiration.

ACKNOWLEDGMENTS

Bapi, my friend, colleague, and coauthor, thanks for all the support and ideas you shared in this effort together. It has always been a great learning experience and fun working with you. I appreciate the trust you have in me and the wisdom you share.

Sincere thanks go to the Apress team for their support, guidance, and assistance during the entire process.

—**Yashajeet Chowdhury**

Introduction

This book aims to provide a 360-degree view of disaster recovery capabilities on Azure. All critical systems need to be protected against any threats for customer and business data. Although the fundamental building blocks are the same with respect to availability and disaster recovery (DR), the usability and capability of modern cloud-based services make things quite different. Usage of decoupled, modular services to develop applications can sometimes make a simple scenario very difficult. To achieve the required service-level agreement (SLA), integration, and protection we need to consider new factors. Hence, understanding the building blocks of Azure-based DR services and tools is key for implementing any DR for on-premises or cloud-based applications.

In this book, we will explore various aspects of planning, designing, and configuring a robust DR solution on Azure. We will also look at a few real-world scenarios that will provide more practical insights.

We will begin with understanding the overall landscape of DR and how cloud technologies have changed the factors to consider. We will explain what Microsoft Azure has to offer in terms of DR and explore various related concepts. We will then dive into the available tools, supportability matrix, and scenarios. Using this information, we will try to develop a scenario-based DR solution. We will look deeper into various cloud-only and hybrid scenarios at the infrastructure and application levels. We will conclude our journey with added automation and monitoring.

This book aims to build from the very basics to the important building blocks of different Azure-based services within a DR context. It aims to cater to a wide audience, ranging from consultants and architects to Azure administrators with beginner to moderate-level Azure knowledge who would like to build their knowledge on scenario-based DR solutions. Happy learning!

Disclaimer

In this book we explore the disaster recovery aspect of business continuity and how Microsoft Azure services and tools help us achieve that. It is important to understand that the topics and concepts discussed in this book are intended to provide high-level guidance and information only. The topics discussed in the book should not be considered the only aspects, perspectives, or considerations that lead you to achieve a suitable level of DR solution for you or your customers.

CHAPTER 1

Disaster Recovery: Background

The world of business continuity is constantly evolving with the ever-changing world of technologies. Cloud technologies have opened a whole new world of possibilities and aspects. Every organization, those of all different sizes and in every industry, is concerned with data and business continuity. The slightest glitch in a system that could result in crucial data loss can cause severe business losses and a negative end-user experience. Hence, every information technology (IT) professional, software developer, architect, consultant, and implementation specialist shares this concern. Business continuity can also be considered a separate practice due to the nature of the work. Things do go wrong and will go wrong. When something does go wrong, though, what proactive and reactive measures can one take to protect and recover when disaster strikes? These are a few questions and principles that business continuity builds on and a careful strategic approach needs to be taken to address them. It is important to understand that business continuity is not limited to software or IT infrastructure architecture; it is an end-to-end process to ensure that business can stay in action. In several industries it is a compliance need as well, and you might just lose customer trust and go out of business if you fail audit compliance. The process encompasses planning, designing, and implementing against anything and everything that can cause a negative impact on your data that

© Bapi Chakraborty and Yashajeet Chowdhury 2020
B. Chakraborty and Y. Chowdhury, *Introducing Disaster Recovery with Microsoft Azure*,
https://doi.org/10.1007/978-1-4842-5917-7_1

could result in a business loss. Examples, include power, cooling systems, software design, security compromises, infrastructure failures, or any other political, health, or environmental issue at the local, regional, or global level.

In this book, we discuss different recovery solutions for IT infrastructure and software systems. We will also share our design perspectives on recovery solutions for various scenarios. We specifically look at how Microsoft Azure and its various services can be leveraged to design a resilient deployment architecture and create a robust recovery solution. You will be able to leverage Microsoft Azure for achieving your recovery objectives for critical applications.

This chapter explores the following topics:

1. Fundamentals of disaster recovery (DR).

2. IT challenges.

3. Modern applications, cloud migration, and DR.

4. How Microsoft Azure technologies enable such constructs.

Fundamentals of Disaster Recovery

Simply put, DR involves restoring the predetermined functionalities of a system within a specific period of time to a point in time prior to the disaster by executing a defined set of actions by specific individuals. In this statement there are five important segments that we should focus on.

- *Predetermined functionalities*: This involves identifying and deciding well ahead of time what features, functions, data, or parts of the system need to be up and running to support the business. In most scenarios, an organization requires a risk assessment of the system and definition of the business-critical functions that are required to be functioning.

- *Specific period of time*: This is also known as the recovery time objective (RTO). This is the amount of time within which the system needs to be back online. In other words, the business can only sustain failure of the system for this defined span of time.

- *Point in time*: This is the point in time to which the system should be recovered to minimize business losses. This is also known as the recovery point objective (RPO).

- *Defined sets of actions*: This involves defining all actions that need to happen either in an automated way or manually to achieve the objectives, including what tools are to be used, how, and at what time.

- *Specific individuals*: In most cases these are named individuals, defined teams and owners who will perform specific tasks to make things happen. It also involves any partners, vendors, and support staff for ensuring appropriate actions are taken by each owner to recover the business system.

As you can see, the entire thing is a process and each segment cannot be looked at in isolation. DR involves establishing a proper plan that involves people, process, and technology. It involves a great deal of effort and time. Let us now look at some of the core concepts and processes involved.

Definition

In discussing all this, an interesting question that we often miss is this: How do you define a disaster and when do you initiate a recovery process? Unless there is absolute objectivity and clarity of vision, a plan will fail because it will not be aligned to business requirements. The following reasons are among the most common for failure.

1. Hardware failures such as disks, computing resources, and so on.

2. Datacenter level failures with power or network switches.

3. Regional failures including uncontrollable incidents such as floods, earthquakes, and so on.

4. Deletion or corruption, faulty writes, malware, ransomware, or hardware issues.

5. Dependency failures; internal or external service reliability issues such as name resolution.

6. Performance-related issues, including peak load or sudden usage increases.

7. Deployment failures; wrong packages, incorrect parameters, and configuration issues.

8. Transient issues, such as network failures, disk read issues, or latency.

Remember that DR is a reactive action. Hence, defining when, how, and why is crucial. For example, we have a simple two-tier public-facing application involving Load Balancer, Web Application Firewall, virtual machines (VMs) hosting Web applications, and a database. The primary objective is to ensure that all resources should be recovered within four hours (RTO) and all functionalities no more than two hours (RPO) prior to the disaster should be recovered. The app can only sustain an outage of up to one hour to minimize severe business losses; outages longer than this are not acceptable. Because failure of any part of the system will potentially cause an application failure, all systems should be highly available and have to be recovered within one hour. It will be a disaster if the outage period is potentially more than one hour and a recovery process has to be initiated.

Events

We react to events. Events can be categorized as controllable or uncontrollable. *Controllable* events are those events for which we can take certain preventive and proactive actions to completely avoid or minimize failures, such as building redundancy into the plan and creating high availability (HA) infrastructure and proactive maintenance. *Uncontrollable* events are not within our control and we need to plan accordingly. Examples would include an earthquake or an Internet service provider (ISP) system failure. Based on those definitions, we can classify several failure points that would make a web portal completely unavailable.

- All database servers being down is a controllable event.

- All web front-end servers being down is a controllable event.

- All Web Application Servers (WAF) being down is a controllable event.

- A complete storage or network outage, resulting from a power outage making the infrastructure unavailable is an uncontrollable event.

- A regional failure due to natural calamities, a missile attack, or a meteorite strike is an uncontrollable event.

- A problem due to a third-party issue (e.g., DNS service provider) is an uncontrollable event.

Based on these events, when should we initiate DR? Here are a few scenarios.

- All necessary steps should be taken to restore the service within the first hour; if that is not successful, declare a DR.

- Onboard your existing practice and experience to this process.

- It takes one hour bring the DR site up and restore the service (by way of a DR drill).

How will we identify if servers and services are down? This is where a robust and well-planned monitoring system comes into play. Monitoring applications for failures, exceptions, and security events is not new. However, implementing a system that can help you decide what failed, when it failed, and what the next steps are should be the key. Because critical applications are required to be available and recovered with minimal service disruptions, the end-to-end process should include a robust monitoring system. Sources that could indicate a failure or outage situation could include one or more of the following:

- Monitoring system alerts.

- Manual testing and identification.

- Service provider outage indication.

- Information from any other third party to the solution (DNS service provider, etc.).

Identify the Requirements

As technology has become more complex, so have the ways in which it can malfunction. Consequently, DR planning has also become more complex, as interruption of service or loss of data can have a serious financial impact, some of which could result from loss of customer confidence. The DR decision comes into the picture when we want to avoid any major regional outage or service outages. This solution eventually gives us the ability to achieve infrastructure or services availability by spinning up the services somewhere else in another geographical area. This is a measurement to define resiliency.

As discussed briefly earlier, there are major metrics and factors such as RTO, RPO, and mean time to recovery (MTTR), that systems can use to restore business operations following a disaster using variations and combinations. Let us discuss them briefly.

- *RTO*: The RTO is the maximum acceptable time that an application can be unavailable after an incident occurs. For example, if the RTO is unavailable for more than 30 minutes, we must be able to restore the application to a running state within 30 minutes from the start of a disaster. In the case of low RTO, we must have a warm standby running a DR site to protect against any outage.

- *RPO*: The RPO is the maximum duration of data loss that is acceptable during a disaster. If you take a database backup or application of file servers each hour, then the RPO stands at 60 minutes.

- *MTTR*: This metric considers the average time that it takes to restore applications after failure. If the MTTR exceeds the RTO, then a failure in the system will cause unacceptable business disruption.

- *Mean time between failures (MTBF)*: The MTBF is how long a component can reasonably expect to last between outages. Use these measures to determine where to add redundancy and to determine service-level agreements (SLAs) for customers.

- *SLAs*: If you are a service provider and take care of the application systems or infrastructure, DR also takes into account the SLA to define DR requirements.

- *Compliance requirements*: Compliance requirements also influence the values of RPO and RTO. Hence, it is important to gather information relating to compliance.

- *Functional and nonfunctional requirements*: Before developing a DR strategy and plan, we should carefully consider the functional and nonfunctional requirements during the outage period and postrecovery. For example, it might be sustainable that the web application is read-only, and users can access their existing data; however, they are unable to write or update new information. The design of the DR infrastructure and the application functionality changes based on this decision and DR planning and implementation can be very different based on such requirements. Similarly, another application might only require specific crucial functionalities to be working and not all the modules to be functional during postrecovery for seven days. If the system does not recover by then, a complete recovery with all functionalities is required at the target or secondary site. This is again a different requirement and planning and implementation will be different.

Develop a Strategy

In putting together a DR strategy, we must envision a set of potential scenarios and outline the appropriate response steps for each scenario. Just having a DR plan is not enough. We must also find a way to test the strategy without putting live operations at risk of interruption. In a traditional datacenter environment, we used to have a DR site where at least once annually we performed the DR drill as a test.

Key factors in determining the DR strategy for an application business system can vary based on the application type. However, the considerations should include both IT systems and non-IT systems. The following are some of examples of such considerations.

- *Identify critical systems.* These could be, for example, payments or manufacturing systems, or whatever is critical to your business. Inherent to the process of identifying these systems is to give them some degree of priority in terms of level of protection or recovery. As part of this discovery, all internal and external dependencies of the application, integration points, and accessibility options should be identified because the same systems have to be set up or accessible postrecovery.

- *Decide on RTOs and RPOs for each system.* How soon do they need to be recovered? This can range from no acceptable level of downtime to periods of minutes or hours in which you can get them up and running again. How much data can you lose, in time terms? Must you restore to exactly where things left off, or is there some leeway?

- *Identify potential threats to each system, or to groups of systems.* These can range from buildings taken out by floods or fire, to incidents that affect individual systems, such as hardware failure or ransomware infection.

- *Develop a prevention strategy.* This addresses the identified threats. Responses could be anything from better flood defenses to and upgraded uninterruptible power source (UPS), to improved server and application protection.

- *Develop a response strategy.* This outlines exactly what needs to happen in case of identified threats causing an outage. This might include failing over to alternative sites or hardware and would be executed with reference to the RPOs and RTOs specified.

- *People.* Questions you'll need to ask in this area might include the following: What is the availability of staff or contractors who might be needed in key areas when implementing DR plans? What training will we need to arrange for them? You might also need to ensure some duplication of critical skills so there can be a primary and a backup person in key areas. Identify the suppliers and service providers who need to be involved at the time of recovery and restoration of the system in the new target location.

- *Assess the target location or premises.* Questions to ask here might include the following: Are there alternate work areas on the same site? Do you need to arrange for the use of different company locations, third-party sites, employees' homes, or temporary buildings? What is the target location for the system? Is it at the same site, same datacenter, same city, same country, or a different country? If the recovery location is another physical location, datacenter setup and protection that duplicate the primary location must be considered.

Along similar lines, for the software or IT infrastructure, similar network, storage, computing, software inventory, connectivity, accessibility, security, and protection capabilities are required to be planned as part of the strategy. For our purposes in this book, we primarily focus on the application business system and its dependent infrastructure pieces.

- *Outline the key tasks required.* Finally, a response strategy will outline the key tasks required to bring systems back to their primary locations with all protections in place against future outages.

Based on the requirements identified, the following topologies and strategies can be adopted for your application DR planning. Note that each application can have a different strategy and a different plan.

- *Redeploy*: In this case, the application is redeployed from scratch at the time of disaster. This is appropriate for noncritical applications that don't require a guaranteed RTO.

- *Backup and restore*: This involves taking backups of the system (e.g., databases, files, virtual machines) and restoring them in a different physical location following a disaster. The frequency of the backups is based on the RPO and will take more time to restore, affecting the RTO. As part of the strategy, backups might be retained in an offsite location hundreds of miles away from the primary location, and only recent backups are kept in the same location. Although it varies from application to application, most organizations invest heavily in this strategy.

- *Lite touch*: In this model, only the core elements of the applications are deployed, and the rest are planned for automated deployment at the time of the disaster. This requires advanced configurations to ensure the recovered infrastructure is built up appropriately and quickly. Our Web application with Web front end, database, WAF, and load balancer will contain only a database deployed in the secondary or target location; the remaining application components can be built through automation. One thing that we need to consider is the application type. Not all applications might support such configuration and could be very difficult to set up with custom code updates, configuration updates, and VM stickiness resulting in higher RTO.

- *Warm/active-passive/standby*: In this case, a scaled-down version of a fully functional environment that is always running in a different location is deployed and kept in sync to be consistent as per the RPO. This separate location could be just another physical location or datacenter or even a public cloud platform. This alternate site does not receive any production traffic. This deployment model and topology greatly reduces the recovery time. This is appropriate for applications that are not designed to be deployed and handle traffic across multiple sites or regions.

- *Hot/active-active/hot-spare/multisite*: This can be considered for scenarios in which the application is designed to work in a multiregional deployment model. The application can be deployed in two or more sites using this model. All locations can be used in an active-active manner and all systems are kept in sync with advanced configurations. The application traffic can be distributed across these environments. This model helps reduce recovery time but requires heavy investment. Figure 1-1 depicts various recovery methods and topologies and their relative cost vs. RPO and RTO attainments.

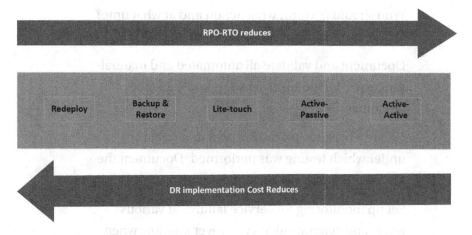

Figure 1-1. *Recovery methods*

Create a Plan

A recovery plan requires careful validation and testing to ensure that all aspects of the application are addressed. A plan should account for the following factors.

1. The business impact of the application in case of failures, severity level, and areas of impact (e.g., data loss, customer confidence loss, only outage, application consistency issues, etc.).

2. Failure possibility. The application could fail for various reasons. A careful validation is required to ensure all possible failures and all possibilities are accounted for, including both controllable and uncontrollable events.

3. Choose the appropriate target region, topology, or strategy for the recovery (hot, warm, cold, etc.).

4. Who should perform what action and at what time? Define owners, responsibilities, and tasks.

5. Document and validate all automated and manual processes, including exact steps and expected outcomes.

6. Create a backup and testing plan and scenarios under which testing was performed. Document the test results and good backup dates.

7. Set up monitoring for service failures at various levels and generate alerts wherever possible when causing outages. Notify and raise service incidents as required.

8. Train each owner to execute the plan.

9. Perform DR drills at regular intervals.

10. Update and record any deviations.

The recovery plan will be different for different applications. It can be anything from a simple Microsoft Excel file to a 100-page document with exhaustive details. The more the detailed the plan is, is the easier it will be to execute. It should include both HA and DR methods. *Resiliency* is the ability of infrastructure to recover from failure and continue functioning by responding to any failure that occurs, which can help to avoid any downtime or data loss. The two core components of resiliency are HA and DR. HA and DR together increase the resiliency of your application and infrastructure.

Preventive and Reactive Plans

Planning for HA is a preventive measure to avoid failures. HA tries to ensure that data will be available to all a very large proportion of the time. This gets measured in percentage of uptime or number of nines; for example, 99.999% or 99.95%, which means data will almost always be available to the users. On the other hand, DR is a process of getting back to an available state. Hence, it can be considered a reactive plan.

If we look deeper, we find that HA is achieved by creating redundancy as part of the design. For example, you determine that your web application will require at least two web servers and two database servers to function in an HA configuration. In this case, the web servers can be configured behind a load balancer and the databases can be clustered. This will protect the workload against any hardware-level failures and ensure that user will always have access to the data. In certain scenarios, it is possible that the user transaction will fail, but it can be processed by resubmitting the same request. In an HA configuration, in the event of a failure in either node in any layer of the application, the requests can be handled by the other surviving node. For databases, various methods such as log shipping, mirroring, and so on, help us to achieve HA. In addition, a proper system state backup and database backups of the systems will help recover data if there are multiple failures, an entire datacenter failure, or a power failure in which systems cannot be restarted. We need to decide whether a backup will suffice to meet the RPO and RTO. If this application requires always-on capability and cannot sustain any outage or loss of data, we should implement an active-active deployment across at least two datacenters or locations, keeping the data in sync at the database level at all times.

Questions to Ask

Whether existing or new, each application will have its own sets of
questions for discovering recovery requirements. For a new application,
it is more of a design plan from the ground up, whereas for an existing
application it is more about understanding the existing application first.
Table 1-1 provides a set of sample questions that we can use.

Table 1-1. *Sample Questions for Your Application*

Sr. No.	Questions	Priority	Response	Owner	Response by Date
1	What is the existing overall communication flow of the application? Who talks to whom and how?	High			
2	How is the current solution interconnected across different environments (Development– Test– User Acceptance Test (UAT)–Production)?	High			
3	What are the various internal and external endpoints that will continue to exist postrecovery?	High			
4	What are the various new internal and external endpoints before and postrecovery?	High			
5	How are these internal and external endpoints are accessed?	High			

(continued)

Table 1-1. (*continued*)

Sr. No.	Questions	Priority	Response	Owner	Response by Date
6	What is the current size of data in each layer?	Medium			
7	What is the expected percentage of growth of the data?	Medium			
8	What is the expected percentage of processing increase month over month or year over year?	Low			
9	Can data from one region move to another region? Does General Data Protection Regulation (GDPR) or any other compliance apply?	High			
10	What is the application fault tolerance from millisecond latency/availability of dependent services? How long can it sustain?	Medium			
11	What are the RPO and RTO requirements of the complete solution?	High			
12	Is there a seperate RPO and RTO requirement for each layer?	Low			
13	Which DR strategy will be followed (hot/warm/cold)? Is anything chalked out already based on RPO and RTO?	Medium			

(*continued*)

Table 1-1. (*continued*)

Sr. No.	Questions	Priority	Response	Owner	Response by Date
14	Is backup and restore part of the DR strategy?	Medium			
15	Will we have HA for all environments or production only?	High			
16	Will we have DR for all environments or production only?	High			
17	Have we decided on the regions already for each environment (if applicable)?	High			
18	Do we have any choice preference for any services for DR, replication, backup, or restore functionality?	Medium			
19	When do we trigger a DR? Both planned and unplanned? What is the defined process workflow?	Low			
20	How often should a DR drill be performed in a year? Are such timelines already defined?	Low			
21	If the solution is deployed in more than one region, will it have data pertaining to that region only?	High			

(*continued*)

Table 1-1. (*continued*)

Sr. No.	Questions	Priority	Response	Owner	Response by Date
22	What are the common services that might or will consume or store data across regions? Do specific compliance requirements such as GDPR apply?	High			
23	How long will the DR site be live in the event of an actual DR? Hours or days?	Medium			
24	Will the target region be an active or primary region postfailover (with read/write) or just a read-only copy?	Low			
25	Will the solution be failed back to the same primary region?	Low			
26	If there is an active-active site, are both sites required to be at full capacity?	Medium			
27	Will there be any changes to the recovery solution on how the resources are aligned (connection and communication flow, etc.) right now?	Medium			

(*continued*)

Table 1-1. (*continued*)

Sr. No.	Questions	Priority	Response	Owner	Response by Date
28	Will DR be triggered in the event just an application layer failed or the entire solution experienced an outage?	High			
29	How will the supported infrastructure be deployed or made available (Active Directory Domain Services, monitoring, security, logging, maintenance, etc.)?	High			
30	What will be operational acceptance criteria of the HA and DR solution?	High			
31	What will be the network connectivity to the DR region?	High			
32	Are all the resources and its types supported across all selected regions and datacenters?	High			
33	Can the initial size and type of resources on the DR site be lower if applicable (type, plan, tier, size, etc.)?	Medium			

(*continued*)

Table 1-1. (*continued*)

Sr. No.	Questions	Priority	Response	Owner	Response by Date
34	What controllable and uncontrollable events are considered as part of the rules for DR failover?	Medium			
35	What are the various internal and external dependencies of the application or source systems?	High			
36	Are the dependent systems already available at the recovery site? How will the various dependencies be made available postfailover?	High			
37	Is separate DR planning required for the internal and external supportive systems? If yes, what, how, and by whom?	High			
38	What is the priority of failover of the systems; which group goes first, and which ones follow?	High			

Sample Template to Create an Initial Plan

Once the high-level details are captured, an initial plan with the required details should be prepared with the best possible alternative for each component, each region, and each service. Table 1-2 is an example.

Table 1-2. *Sample Template*

Components	Example(s)
Region	Specify the source region or country (e.g., U.S. East, Australia, etc.)
Component that fails	Hardware or a service component, entire datacenter, region, network or data compromise, etc.
Scenario	Service level, instance level, situation, etc.
Failure impact	Website unavailable, user experience
Action timeline	Immediate or wait for *x* hours before initiating DR
Sequence of guidelines for recovery	Redirect, troubleshoot, restore, etc.
Activities required	Activities required based on sequence of choice of previous details
Recovery steps	High-level steps and detailed steps with absolute granularity should be created as a runbook to be followed with each action; for example: 1. Troubleshoot and resolve. 2. Restore from latest or required backup set. 3. Restore from last known good source. 4. Redeploy the instance and recover from backup, source, or reload.
Prerequisites	What must happen to make this work; all prework for this plan
DR process type	Automated, manual, or combination of both
Workflow/decision tree	Specify the recovery workflow and create a document with the entire decision tree

(*continued*)

Table 1-2. (*continued*)

Components	Example(s)
Blockers identified	Any identified blockers
Remediation/ mitigation plan	Remediation plan: Scenario-based plans for each blocker
Owners and contacts	All concerned contacts and corresponding responsibilities
Expected timelines for action	Overall expected or tested timelines for each action in the plan

As you can see, there can be two documents; one is a high-level plan and one is a runbook with each action per scenario, per service, and per solution.

Documents to Review

Whether it is an existing application or a new one, all high-level design documents (HLDs), low-level design documents (LLDs), an application or solution owner interview coupled with an architecture diagram will be required to be reviewed. The as-is state of the solution or application for which the DR has to be planned should be well understood.

Assumed Failure

Assumed failure considers that things will eventually fail, and you should design your application and its underlying infrastructure accordingly so that it can be resilient. Design considerations should include what code-level failures might occur, which application architecture is vulnerable, and how various integration components can be made more reliable to build redundancy of the underlying computing and database platforms. For modern applications, there are new patterns and methods that can be leveraged to develop a robust, resilient, scalable, and highly available application. The following are some examples.

1. Perform failure mode analysis to identify types of failures the application might experience.

2. Build redundancy for each tier and workload to avoid a single point of failure.

3. Design for retries to sustain transient network failures.

4. Implement platform HA capabilities wherever possible.

5. Define a backup and recovery method for each tier of the application.

6. Design an appropriate application data replication method. For example, certain enterprise applications such as SQL Server or Oracle use their own DR methods more reliably.

7. Deploy application consistently, every leveraging DevOps principles.

8. Monitor and respond to application health and infrastructure failures.

9. Perform testing of each design construct, ensuring that the application and the platform design can handle the failures it is designed to handle.

10. Implement appropriate access control for the application and data.

Implement the Actionable

Now that we have a plan and method, it is time to establish and test.

Establish a Pattern

Based on the application type, new or existing, once all the preventive and reactive plans are devised, they need to be tested. However, it is obvious that most large enterprises will have if not thousands, at least a few hundred applications. At times, applications will follow a certain pattern, technologies, deployment model, and owners. Based on such information, it is easier to devise one or multiple DR patterns. All applications that follow a common application construct and deployment model could possibly follow the same DR pattern. For example, all two-tier internal-facing web applications containing a web tier (one server) and a database tier (one server) hosted on IIS (.NET-based stateless application) and SQL Server can follow the same pattern. Let's assume that to attain HA and DR for all two-tier critical applications, they all should sustain datacenter-level failures and RTO and RPO of four and two hours, respectively. Figure 1-2 is a simple web application hosted on IIS and SQL Server database.

Figure 1-2. *Simple web application with SQL back end*

In such a case, because the application front end is stateless and only database connectivity is required, we can develop a pattern that involves the following:

1. At least one web server in the primary datacenters.

2. At least two database servers across two different datacenters

3. Ensuring stable network connectivity across two datacenters.

4. Implementing database replication with an AlwaysOn availability group.

5. Backing up databases daily and transaction logs every two hours.

6. Developing and testing a web tier system template with an operating system and application image for rapid deployment and configuration within two hours.

7. Switching necessary DNS entries to point to the new web server.

8. Implementing application endpoint monitoring for availability.

9. Implementing database and web server monitoring for service health.

10. Generating and logging triggers and notifying necessary contacts on application, web endpoint, and service failures.

This lite touch DR pattern is shown in Figure 1-3.

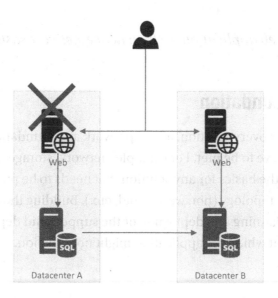

Figure 1-3. *Web application with a lite touch disaster recovery method*

The same pattern can be modified with an additional load balancer service that can serve both web servers across datacenters. This will help both regions to be active at any point in time, as shown in Figure 1-4.

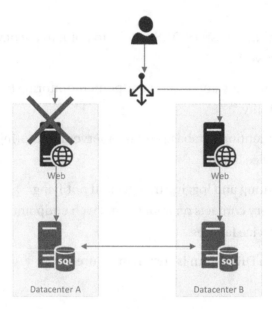

Figure 1-4. *Web application with an active-active disaster recovery method*

Build the Foundation

To deploy the recovery solution, all the prework and foundational requirements have to be met. For example, network, storage, and computing are the basics for any solution that needs to be planned based on the recovery topology (hot, warm, cold, etc.). Building the foundation also includes planning and deploying for the support and dependent systems, without which the application might not function.

Deploy and Test

Once such a solution is deployed, it should be tested by running simulated or orchestrated failures. This might include failover of the database from the primary datacenter to the secondary datacenter, deploying the Web front end application package and configuring the same to access the web server. Everything should be back online and accessible within the RTO hours if such a recovery is initiated. The testing should satisfy the original objectives of developing and deploying such a solution and encompass the entire range of recovery activities for all failure scenarios. It is important to mention that this is where almost all organizations face the biggest challenge. An end-to-end test requires a longer outage window, more people, and more resources. Because traditional solutions did not have enough capability to ensure testing could be achieved without hindering production, not all the scenarios were tested completely. If you want to ensure that your recovery solution works when you need it the most, it must be tested under all scenarios for all components against the RPO and RTO requirements.

IT Challenges

IT faces several unique challenges not only in managing and maintaining the IT infrastructure and applications, but also in ensuring seamless business continuity capabilities. Exponential data growth, heterogeneous systems, unaccounted integration points, and undocumented legacy applications to the latest modern advanced workloads haunt IT management every day. No matter how streamlined and appropriate it might look, there exist an ocean of unknowns when it comes to the entire IT asset portfolio.

1. Business continuity is a complicated process. Complex change control coupled with human errors and rapid changes in technology continue to test IT services to establish and maintain business continuity DR processes.

2. Exponential and rapid data growth and the cost of protecting that data is another unique challenge. Several enterprises only protect their most critical data. In most scenarios they leave tier 2 and tier 3 workloads with little—or even no—protection.

3. Organizations are bound by stringent regulations everyday. Whether it is for data retention, privacy, or security of stored data and on the wire, the IT services world is continuously challenged to meet the desired goal at its best. A longer retention period multiplied by ever-growing data volume results in high costs.

4. Traditionally data backups are managed onsite and offsite. The world is now moving from tape-based backups, which are very cumbersome to manage and maintain, to more reliable hybrid storage options involving cloud storage. The primary issues with tape and media-based backups coupled with offsite storage is the validity of the backup and transporting the media back to the primary location at the time of a disaster in a timely fashion. Owing to the complexity involved, many enterprises do not do enough to test the recovery mechanism. Also, their DR plans are often not regularly validated for consistency. Irregular DR drills and surprises unearth the truth.

5.   Data protection and DR costs grow linearly with the growth of data and the number of applications and VMs.

6.   Adopting and operationalizing newer methods of business continuity solutions continuously is another challenge.

Given these scenarios and challenges, the IT services organizations of each enterprise have started to consider updated options as game changers. Let us look at some of them here.

Automation

Automating all repetitive tasks helps make business continuity plans more reliable. This makes the process human error-free, efficient, and effortless. It also helps to handle the continuous growth of data.

Hybrid Storage

Several organizations have started leveraging hybrid storage options. These solutions integrate with cloud storage, which is much cheaper, more reliable, and easier to use and manage. Such solutions store frequently used data on-premises and less used data to remote cloud-based storage that can be fetched anytime when required. There are also storage-level replication solutions available that help sync primary and secondary storage across different locations. Such solutions help make offsite storage much easier.

Cloud-Based Backup

Cloud-based backup services are now a reality. Various storage options in the cloud (hot, cold, archival) and possible integration with leading backup software helps to back up on-premises and store the data to the cloud. It also helps to perform item-level, snapshot-level recoveries if required, so that IT teams need not worry about storage management, multiple media management, ever increasing growth of data, and the associated costs.

DevOps

Adoption of DevOps and agile methodologies enables administrators to make continuous updates and maintain and restore to a desired state whenever it is required. Streamlined build and release pipelines help to maintain the desired state at all times. It also helps to manage the code without errors and with seamless deployments.

Infrastructure as Code

Whether on-premises or in the cloud, infrastructure as code is a reality today. In the past, adoption of DevOps processes to enable infrastructure as code was very difficult. However, services such as Azure DevOps (ADO) and Amazon Web Services (AWS) have changed that. Infrastructure constructs with predefined templates, codes, and scripts allow you to rapidly deploy and provision the same infrastructures for your application. This has led to new scenarios in recovery processes. Because these templates and constructs allow for consistent, error-free deployment, they allow you to plan, design, and deploy new infrastructure and applications to a new target site and enable a seamless recovery process. Scripts such as PowerShell Desired State scripting with automation help provide a consistent platform every time. Azure Stack, software-defined datacenter technologies, also enable across-site recoveries and reduced RTOs.

Contemporary DR Patterns

As more and more enterprises are adopting and migrating to the cloud, they have started to adopt the cloud-based patterns and best practices, too. This has helped organizations be more agile, resilient, and efficient. Because they are able to test and perform DR drills with greater ease, without affecting production workloads and in a tested manner, the confidence level and trust in the new patterns has increased, too. We will discuss cloud-based Microsoft Azure services and recovery patterns in greater detail in later chapters. Cloud-based DR orchestration is one such option wherein both the primary and secondary datacenters can be either of the on-premises or in the cloud; however, the replication, management, and orchestration of the recovery process is handled through a cloud-based service. Figure 1-5 depicts one such scenario wherein the secondary site is created with replication orchestration and can be brought up online if the primary site is unavailable.

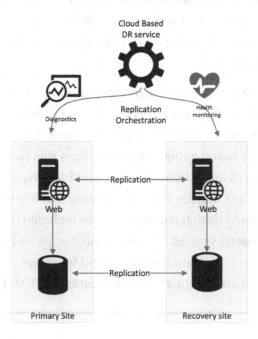

Figure 1-5. *Web application with an active-active disaster recovery method*

Various Applications and Disaster Recovery

Achieving the highest degree of resiliency for critical workloads is a must for modern enterprises. The cloud has changed the way applications are envisioned, designed, developed, deployed, and maintained. Modern applications are more agile, are more resilient, follow end-to-end continuous integration and continuous deployment capabilities, and try to achieve global customer and user bases in the shortest time span. This leads to a new genre of patterns and practices for application design architectures. It is therefore important that the same capabilities are protected and recovered when there is an unforeseen incident, and that the application and all its related data are recovered and restored. Broadly, we can categorize these applications into six types.

1. *Legacy n-tier applications*: The legacy one-, two-, three-, or n-tier applications are hosted on-premises. These can be web based or typical client/server applications. An example is a web application with a SQL database.

2. *Modern applications*: The modern applications that leverage decoupled architecture might or might not leverage cloud technologies. An example is a container-based application or the ones that use a content delivery network and cloud identity. Applications that are born in the cloud and follow cloud-based design patterns are also included in this category, such as an application that processes documents based on file upload and leverages serverless architectures and no computing (VMs).

3. *Rehosted or refactored applications*: The applications are migrated to the cloud as part of datacenter evacuation or exit or as part of an overall modernization effort by the organization. These can be any of the first two, net new or refactored to a different architecture for cost optimization, to bring in cloud scale, resiliency, and availability.

4. *Enterprise workloads*: Enterprise applications and special workloads have built-in disaster recovery capabilities and follows their own DR pattern or require special considerations. Examples include Windows Active Directory, SQL Server, Oracle databases, Microsoft DNS service, Dynamic Host Configuration Protocol (DHCP) service, System Center Suite, Systems Applications and Products (SAP), Virtual Desktop Infrastructure (VDI), and so on. We discuss some of these later in this book.

5. *Industrialized applications*: These are industry-specific specialized or industrial applications. Examples include deep-sea exploration, mining, smart buildings, smart city command control centers, and so on.

6. *Special workloads*: These include applications relating to big data analytics, high-performance computing, or data warehouse systems.

In any of these types, depending on the criticality of the application and the type of data it hosts, a DR plan might exist or might need to be planned. Hence, we can apply the fundamentals of DR to them and explore how cloud services can be leveraged and what considerations must be made.

Introducing Disaster Recovery with Microsoft Azure

Broadly, a conventional DR solution includes the following considerations for the target recovery site of recovery.

- Target a location, including a physical location, building, and personnel for maintaining and managing an additional infrastructural environment.

- Preassess the computing, network, and storage resources you must replicate for apps from your on-premises setup to the secondary DR site.

- Plan, design, implement, and maintain security with respect to both physical and information security.

- RTO and RPO thresholds should be maintained at values as low as possible.

- Continuous replication should be maintained in terms of storage and computing, at the same time maintaining the Input-Output Operations (IOPS) requirements designated for the specific set of applications.

- Plan for and maintain capacity, network bandwidth, network configuration, and daily change rate planning.

- Consider long data-retention requirements.

When you plan and design your systems to recover your critical applications in Microsoft Azure as a secondary site you gain additional resiliency and features that are provided by the Microsoft Azure platform. By leveraging Azure-based tools and services, your recovery implementation can achieve availability in the cloud. Traditionally viewed as only recovery in the cloud, Microsoft breaks this mold and sets a new standard with a*vailability on demand*, which means one should be able to recover the data at any time and the data required to recover is always available. With Microsoft Azure services coupled with platform resiliency, DR has a new look.

Once a connection from your datacenter to Azure is established, your servers are replicated, much like a traditional recovery or backup solution. With your data now in Azure, you not only have the safety net of being able to leverage Azure as a secondary site in a time of need, but you also have unfettered access to the robust computing and storage capacity of Azure. Because your data is already in Azure, standing up a replicated workload in Azure for DevTest, or assigning a larger Azure template to provide additional computing capacity is as simple as a few clicks, and there is no effect to your on-premises production workload. Just as easy as getting your data into Azure is bringing it back on-premises in the same manner, even if you use a physical server or VMware VM. Backing up your data to Azure means you'll never need to invest in additional hardware to back up your exponentially growing data, and with up to 99 years of retention, your regulatory needs are met. We discuss this feature in greater detail in upcoming chapters.

No matter where your systems are (on-premises or in the cloud), one of the essential ingredients is that they are resilient; it has the ability to withstand a failure, whether mild or catastrophic. It should be able to handle not only transient failures, but also failures at multiple levels (specific tier, hardware, or service failure); and when the entire datacenter or the region experiences a failure owing to an uncontrollable event, there should be an effective solution in place that can recover the systems and ensure business continuity as quickly as possible.

If you are developing your application for Microsoft Azure or you are developing a recovery solution for an existing application with Azure as a target secondary location, you should know that you are building your solution at its best. With Microsoft Azure, you have four ways to build resiliency for various types of failures into your application. Awareness of these capabilities and a structured, well-defined plan is key to design recovery for a new or an existing application in the cloud. These four facets are:

- Platform-level resiliency and capabilities.

- Service-level resiliency and capabilities.

- Available tools on Azure and its integration.

- Know-how to use the three facets given to create a resilient design for recovery.

Platform-Level Resiliency

Microsoft Azure provides a host of capabilities to plan, design, and implement recovery capabilities and to make your application resilient. When you start building, realize that you do not have to plan and build the target location from scratch. You can plan for resiliency either at the VM level, datacenter level, or regional level. With service-level SLAs up to 99.99% for your VMs, you can easily design a cost-effective solution. You get an SLA of 99.95% for a single VM solution with premium storage attached. For higher SLAs, plan for redundancy and build at least two VMs for each tier.

To protect against hardware, disk, or network failures, use at least two VMs in an *availability set,* which is a group of VMs that do not share a common power and network switch, hence eradicating a single point of failure.

Leverage *availability zones* to avoid datacenter-wide failures. Each availability zone is a physically separate zone within a Azure region. Each zone contains one or more datacenters that has distinct power, cooling, and network functions. While designing your infrastructure pattern, validate service and zone availability in the target region. Also ensure an application can maintain its state to prevent data loss, has no hard-coded infrastructure components, and supports running in a distributed environment. It is advisable to discuss these features with the vendor, application owner, or developer for such supportability.

Azure has multiple regions in a geopolitical area and each specific region has a corresponding *paired region* to enhance platform resiliency. All planned maintenance on Azure is serialized for one region in the paired set at a time, thereby increasing the overall uptime of the services. This also helps to meet data sovereignty and compliance requirements specific to a geopolitical area. You will find complete details on paired region sets at `https://docs.microsoft.com/en-us/azure/best-practices-availability-paired-regions`.

Service-Level Resiliency

Each service on Azure has certain built-in capabilities to design and deploy for HA and DR. It isn't possible here to discuss all the service-specific details, but we can look at a few examples. Refer to the online documentation available for each of the services on Azure. For VMs, one can leverage the concepts of a single VM SLA, paired region, and availability sets or availability zones. Similarly, for Azure storage services, plan to leverage redundancy features such as locally redundant storage (LRS), zone redundant storage (ZRS), or geo-redundant storage (GRS). On the networking side, application design and deployment should leverage services such as a Web Application firewall with at least two instances, load balancers to distribute traffic across multiple hosts, or an application gateway for advanced routing with built-in resiliency. Similarly, services such as Georeplication for Azure SQL Database and Traffic Manager with nested profiles for global load balancing use at least two instances for Application gateway. Find more about each service resiliency at `https://docs.microsoft.com/en-us/azure/architecture/checklist/resiliency-per-service`.

Tools and Integration

Other than the key components already discussed, the two key services that Microsoft Azure provides are Azure Backup and Azure Site Recovery (ASR). Azure Backup is a backup solution to protect on-premises and cloud-deployed resources. ASR, on the other hand, enables replication of VMs across on-premises and Azure to create an identical copy of resources that can be brought to life online when required during the time of a disaster. It can also integrate with SQL AlwaysOn Availability groups for failover and failback by creating DR plans. It complements other application-level replication technologies such as Exchange database availability groups and Windows Active Directory replication. We discuss this in greater detail in our next chapter.

Know-How

This is the ingredient that glues everything together. A lot of effort goes into this small but critical part. How do we tie all the capabilities together to create a resilient DR solution? This is something that comes by understanding what is available, what is possible, integrations, experiments, and experiences. We explore this key element as we move through the upcoming chapters in this book.

Summary

In this chapter we discussed in detail and explored the fundamentals of DR, key elements, and how things might go wrong in several ways. We also looked at the key actions required to define, plan, design, and develop a good recovery plan. Resiliency is achieved when a solution is planned and built from the ground up and at every layer of the solution, from the application design and infrastructure design to leveraging all possible platform features that provide resiliency. We discussed how modern cloud-based services and solutions can address modern IT challenges and provide ease of management and monitoring. We also explored Azure platform capabilities, service capabilities, and tools available such as Azure Site Recovery and Azure Backup, and its integration possibilities. In the next chapter, we dive deeper into these tools and capabilities and learn more with scenario-based examples. We will start with the basics of ASR.

CHAPTER 2

Introducing Azure Site Recovery

Azure Site Recovery (ASR) is one of the most prominent and highly regarded DR services offered by Azure for use in cloud and hybrid cloud architectures. ASR is the only available DR platform that makes it possible for Azure VMs, Hyper-V, physical on-premises systems, and VMware to fail over to and successfully fail back once a disaster has resolved. Microsoft Azure Site Recovery is the only public cloud solution that offers a native DR solution for applications running on Internet as a Service (IaaS) VMs. ASR helps to reduce costs by eliminating secondary datacenters and large, up-front third-party software purchases with complex learning curves. ASR is very simple to deploy and easy to manage, as you can administer it entirely through the Azure portal and using Azure Site Recovery PowerShell.

The ASR solution provides several advantages in decision making, planning, and execution to help set up infrastructure DR capabilities far beyond what we were able to achieve with a traditional approach. ASR provides a heterogeneous environment, meaning that it can work on different environments, workload-aware, and on an architecture that is safe with a guarantee of service on the public cloud.

© Bapi Chakraborty and Yashajeet Chowdhury 2020
B. Chakraborty and Y. Chowdhury, *Introducing Disaster Recovery with Microsoft Azure*,
https://doi.org/10.1007/978-1-4842-5917-7_2

ASR can help us to effectively handle most of the issues we face in the case of conventional DR. Some of the benefits that makes this solution able to address nearly all challenges are the following.

- It is a highly scalable solution in both aspects of vertical and horizontal scaling by integrating or adding required computing resources.

- It has a highly affordable pay-as-you-go pricing model; you pay only for the computing services you are going to use for DR.

- There is no need to build a secondary physical site and invest effort and money to buy any additional hardware and software to provide high-end support for all critical operations.

- You can perform DR in an instant from anywhere with a bare minimum requirement of having an Internet-connected device.

- You can back up all your data and store it across multiple Azure regions, which helps to eliminate single points of failure. This will always allow us to have a backup copy available, even if one of the cloud datacenters fails.

- Its better network infrastructure design ensures that any issues or errors that occur can be identified and taken care of by Azure.

- Its automated test recovery ensures your data will be recovered accurately by simulating the failover scenario on a test failover network that will not affect the production environment and perform the testing in a nondisruptive mode.

- The RPO determines the amount of time between data backups, therefore setting the maximum amount of data that might be lost.

- The RTO –sets the maximum amount of time that can elapse before you must have your data restored.

- Data protection provides additional security to protect your backup data from viruses and ransomware.

- Finally, Azure ensures 24/7 technical support and maintenance of storage, including hardware and software upgrades.

Traditional vs. Azure Site Recovery

Chapter 1 covered the importance of having business continuity and DR in place in the IT world. We also learned all the possible ways to move toward a better, stronger, and more sustainable productive infrastructure DR environment solution. Now let's us turn to the outstanding capabilities of ASR as compared to a conventional DR solution.

Conventional Datacenter Disaster Recovery

Before the cloud came into existence or more precisely before ASR came to be, we used to follow a standard workable approach to DR solutions. This includes numerous factors to consider and maintain: cost, security, storage, archiving, maintenance, and accessibility.

Back in the 1990s, traditional siloed datacenters became popular, and by the year 2000 demand was high due to the dot-com boom. First let's examine the challenges, constraints, rigidity, and finally the brainstorming we used to provide substantial solutions in the era of traditional datacenter IT business continuity and DR solutions.

IT teams across the globe faced many challenges in maintaining their business continuity capabilities. A primary challenge was high data growth rates, which created numerous problems, including the complex process of load balancing workloads between storage systems and application performance consistency. If systems are running out of capacity, that can lead to downtime if not proactive measures are not taken, which can further affect business continuity by causing application performance issues.

Before cloud solutions emerged, with conventional datacenters, we had to consider many aspects to provide effective solutions for the business continuity and DR requirements of any organization. The following elements were factors in the siloed datacenter approach to DR.

- Selection of the right physical location, building, and resources to maintain and manage an additional infrastructural environment.

- Preassessing the computing, network, and storage resources you need to replicate apps from your on-premises setup to the secondary DR site.

- Totally relying on physical servers and hardware, which led to inefficient architectures and slow delivery solutions.

- Maintaining the security of both physical and information security.

- RTO and RPO thresholds to maintain as low as possible.

- Capacity, network bandwidth, network configuration, and daily change rate planning and maintenance.

- Business continuity is a combination of complicated processes, complex change control, and human errors. Solutions for this are challenging to establish, and even more challenging to maintain.

- Extremely rapid data growth of data that could be around 40% annually, meaning that the cost of protecting that data was also growing at the same rate.

- The challenges of not only protecting the most critical data, but also to adequately protecting the tier 2 and tier 3 workloads as well.

- Length of retention multiplied by fast-growing data sizes results in greater expenses.

- Some organizations used tapes, which require more time to manage properly and often involve both onsite and offsite media management, incurring additional costs.

- Many organizations fail to test recoveries of their backups and many don't test their DR plans regularly to ensure that solutions in place are up to date and result in rapid restoration of service.

- Most of the costs for data protection and DR grow linearly with the growth of data and number of applications or VMs.

Azure Site Recovery

Microsoft offers a consistent platform so that you can choose to run workloads where it makes sense for your business: in your datacenter, in a service provider's datacenter, or in Microsoft Azure.

ASR breaks the traditional mold of DR and sets a new standard with availability on demand. It provides a single DR solution that works across platforms (Hyper-V, VMware, physical), across clouds (public, private, and those of other service providers), across workloads, and even in case of protecting infrastructure that is already on Azure (Azure-to-Azure recovery) to provide a range of RTO and RPO using multiple channels. We are going to discuss in detail each of these scenarios, starting with Azure-to-Azure recovery in the next section.

ASR features that contribute to your application-level protection and recovery strategy include the following.

- Near-synchronous replication with RPOs as low as 30 seconds to meet the needs of most critical applications.

- App-consistent snapshots for single or n-tier applications.

- Integration with SQL Server AlwaysOn, and partnership with other application-level replication technologies, including Active Directory replication, SQL AlwaysOn, Exchange Database Availability Groups (DAGs), and Oracle Data Guard.

- Flexible recovery plans that enable you to recover an entire application stack with a single click and include external scripts or manual actions.

- Advanced network management in Site Recovery and Azure that simplifies network requirements for an app, including reserving IP addresses, configuring load balancers, or integration of Azure Traffic Manager for low RTO network switchovers.

- A rich automation library that provides production-ready, application-specific scripts that can be downloaded and integrated with Site Recovery.

Once we are able to establish the connection from datacenter to Azure, servers are ready to be replicated, much like a traditional recovery or backup solutions. After the data gets replicated in Azure, not only do you have the network of redundancy and the safety net of being able to leverage Azure as a secondary site in a time of need, but you also have unlimited access to the robust computing and storage capacity solution of Azure, which will keep the data safe and secure via a continuous replication process as a part of ASR.

As your data is already in Azure, standing up a replicated workload in Azure for DevTest, or assigning a larger Azure template to provide additional computing capacity is as simple as a few clicks, with no impact for the on-premises production workload.

It is just as easy to get your data back in Azure is bringing it back on premises in the same manner, even if it is a physical server or any other hypervisor-based VMs. Availability on demand goes beyond traditional IT challenges and seamlessly connects and extends Microsoft's on-premises solutions into Azure. Instead of leveraging multiple solutions, attached to a mix of private and public clouds, Microsoft provides an unmatched integration of on-premises assets with Azure in one solution. Whether an environment has physical, Hyper-V, or VMware assets, with availability on demand, the power of Azure is just a few clicks away.

Incorporating the replication, failover, and failback, ASR gives flexibility to businesses to orchestrate, automate, and manage workloads that are located in Azure VMs and on-premises VMs to create customized DR plans. The following are the main components of the ASR process.

- *Replication*: By synchronizing the contents of your operating systems and the disks of your servers or VMs, ASR helps to move your workloads, including apps, from a primary site datacenter to a secondary site datacenter (in the case of Azure it will be a region) hosted on either Azure or an on-premises environment.

- *Failover*: If an outage affects the primary site, you can access workloads and use apps from your secondary location seamlessly.

- *Failback*: When the primary site is back up and operational again, ASR helps by giving you the flexibility to fail back to its primary site seamlessly. In this case, the delta changes will get replicated back to the primary site and will help to get the primary site up and running from the state of the changes that happened until the thorough failback.

When it comes to reliability, ASR meets ISO 27001:2013, 27018, HIPAA, DPA certified, SOC2, and FedRAMP assessments. ASR is also backed by a 99.9% SLA and 24/7 support to ensure the business will remain up and running when a disaster happens, so customers will be ready to maintain full functionality of their IT environment.

Supported Scenarios

From enterprises to small and medium businesses, all have a common need to have highly reliable DR applications in place catering to end users 24/7. If look deeper into that before addressing application HA, we even have requirements for complex scenarios that are placed across different types of hosting environments. These scenarios can fall primarily into categories like physical boxes-based hosting multitier applications or virtualized-based infrastructure hosting multitier applications across different platforms. To provide a DR solution for such a wide range of heterogenous environments, we need something like a magic wand. It would be ideal to have one solution that can work for several or all of the different hosting scenarios.

To keep pace with the dynamically changing IT space and accelerate enterprise processes across on-premises and cloud environments, it is essential to have better methods to unlock new and faster ways to solve and prevent problems, streamline operations, and help improve service and agility.

This highlights the importance of ASR, which can provide a wide range of scenario-based solutions that can address challenges to providing heterogenous infrastructure-based applications DR solution from enterprises to small and medium businesses.

Next we review all the supported scenarios that ASR can address.

Scenario 1: Azure-to-Azure ASR

Microsoft Azure offers an option to replicate VMs from one geographical region to another. For example, VMs hosted in the East U.S. Azure datacenter can be replicated to the West U.S. or Western Europe and you can achieve a highly reliable DR solution within the native Azure cloud. When the ASR DR solution is deployed for your Azure infrastructure, all selected VMs on Azure can continuously replicate from the hosted region to a different target region. If any unexpected outage occurs or there is a planned or test failover, your selected infrastructure will be able to fail over VMs to the secondary region. Users will be able to access them from the secondary region without having major downtime or loss of productivity. Once the primary datacenter infrastructure starts running normally again, you can fail back and continue working in the primary location. The architecture shown in Figure 2-1 gives a graphic interpretation of how the Azure application infrastructure in one region protected by ASR can be available for end users when a disaster takes place. As you can see, there is an application infrastructure in the East U.S. region having a database server, three app servers, and web servers running Apache or for any web hosting platform. All these are part of a virtual network along with a shared storage account. As you can see, the East US infrastructure is replicated by ASR to the West U.S. region. Now when an actual disaster occurs or a planned failover happens, the whole West U.S. infrastructure will be triggered. During this episode, the end user continue to be served as expected. The key observation here is the continuous replication between the East U.S. and West U.S. datacenters, which ASR handles for us to keep our infrastructure in sync between the two Azure regions.

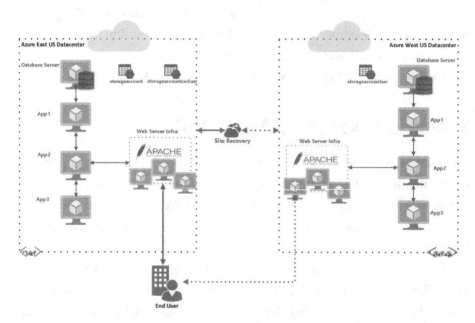

Figure 2-1. *Azure-to-Azure disaster recovery*

Scenario 2: On-Premises Physical Infrastructure or VMware Infrastructure to Azure ASR

Let us now take the environment just discussed and see how ASR works for a end-to-end cloud-based business continuity DR solution for our local application infrastructure servers. ASR works seamlessly by putting together 24/7 replication synchronization to facilitate automatic recovery from on-premises outages. As part of protecting our on-premises physical infrastructure to Azure, we have to set up the configuration server, create a replication policy, and select the servers that need to be protected. Before moving ahead, we need to understand the roles of configuration, process, and master target servers.

- *Configuration server*: This role server helps to coordinate communications between on-premises resources and Azure and manages data replication.

- *Process server*: This role gets installed by default on the configuration server and it helps in receiving replication data; optimizes it with caching, compression, and encryption; and sends it to Azure Storage. The role server also installs Mobility Service on VMs that we want to replicate and performs automatic discovery.

- *Master target server*: This role also gets installed by default on the configuration server and helps to handle replication data during failback from Azure.

All of the selected servers will be synced to a cache storage account. These servers can stay online at the on-premises environment while the changes are constantly being written to Azure. Once an initial copy of the server data is replicated to Azure storage, replication of changes to Azure begins on your server. The initial sync might take some time, depending on your Internet connection. ASR will replicate data over a public endpoint (Internet). We can also throttle the bandwidth of the configuration server to minimize impact on your company network. Figure 2-2 showcases the typical scenario of an on-premises physical/VMware VM DR to Azure.

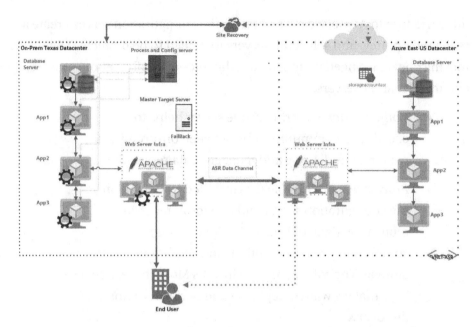

Figure 2-2. *On-premises physical or VMware infrastructure to Azure ASR*

When you have a scenario to deploy DR replication, failover, and recovery of VMware VMs between an on-premises VMware site and Azure using the ASR service, you can use similar considerations with a small change in approach. For DR of on-premises VMware VMs, we have to install and run the configuration server as an on-premises, highly available VMware VM. It is recommended that we deploy the configuration server using a downloaded Open Virtual Appliances (OVA) template from Azure Portal. If for any reason we are unable to deploy a VMware VM using an OVA template, then we can set up the configuration server machines manually.

While setting up disaster recovery for VMware VMs and physical servers using ASR, in the process of enabling the protection it will install the Site Recovery Mobility Service on each on-premises VMware VM and physical server. This service is responsible for capturing data writes on the machine and forwarding them to the Site Recovery process server as shown in Figure 2-3.

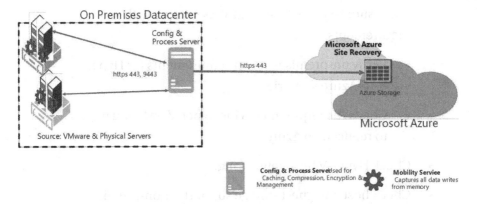

Figure 2-3. Mobility Service, process, and configuration service relation

---

Note   We can use the same constructs to migrate AWS VMs to Azure VMs using ASR. The only trick in this process is that when you migrate AWS EC2 instances to Azure, the VMs are treated like physical, on-premises computers.

Scenario 3: Hyper-V Infrastructure Without Virtual Machine Manager to Azure ASR

We can also have an environment where we have the application servers running on Hyper-V-based VMs. In such scenarios, ASR can again provide a seamless DR infrastructure setup option, as shown in Figure 2-4. We need to prepare the on-premises Hyper-V infrastructure when we want to set up DR of Hyper-VMs to Azure using ASR. Before we proceed, we must check a few things very cautiously.

- Make sure Hyper-V hosts and VMs comply with requirements.

  - Verify on-premises server requirements for Hyper-V-to-Azure scenario.

  - Check the requirements for Hyper-V VMs you want to replicate to Azure.

- Check Hyper-V host networking.

- Check host and guest storage support for on-premises Hyper-V hosts.

- Compare the supported configuration for Azure networking, storage, and computing, after failover.

- We must comply with Azure VM requirements before planning on-premises VMs we want to replicate to Azure.

- Verify Internet access.

We should install the ASR Provider and Azure Recovery Services Agent on each stand-alone Hyper-V host, or on each Hyper-V cluster node. The Provider is responsible to orchestrate replication with ASR over the Internet and the Recovery Services Agent handles data replication. The communications between both the Provider and the Agent are secure and encrypted, and the replicated data in Azure storage is also encrypted.

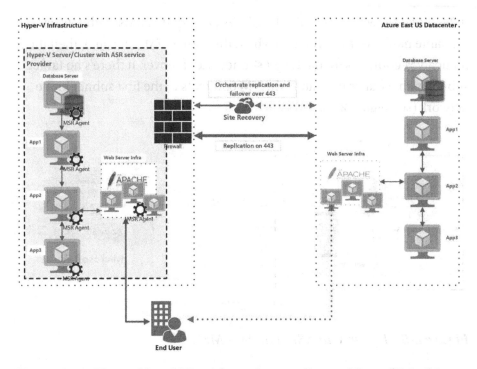

Figure 2-4. *Hyper-V to ASR without System Center Virtual Machine Manager*

Scenario 4: Hyper-V Infrastructure with Virtual Machine Manager to Azure ASR

In some scenarios, customers might have a System Center Configuration Manager as virtualization management (SCVMM/VMM) solution deployed in the datacenter for enhanced virtualized environment management. To address such scenarios and to enable replication for on-premises Hyper-V VMs managed by System Center Virtual Machine Manager (VMM) and for DR to Azure, we can use the ASR service.

We map a source VMM VM network to an Azure virtual network. After failover, Azure VMs in the source network will be connected to the mapped target virtual network. New VMs added to the source VM network are connected to the mapped Azure network when replication occurs.

If the target network has multiple subnets, and one of those subnets has the same name as the subnet on which the source VM is located, then the replica VM connects to that target subnet after failover. If there's no target subnet with a matching name, the VM connects to the first subnet in the network (see Figure 2-5).

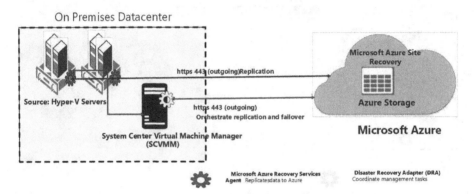

Figure 2-5. *Hyper-V to ASR with SCVMM*

Deprecated Scenario: On-Premises Primary Site VMware/Physical Server Replication to Secondary Physical Site ASR

This scenario is deprecated in terms of future Microsoft ASR support, but for existing customers who implemented this scenario before August 2018, it will be supported until the end of 2020. This scenario was addresses the requirement of customers that have both physical or VMware-based primary and secondary sites that they want to protect. In such a scenario, ASR is a boon for IT business continuity DR decision makers. They can decide when and how to set up DR replication, failover, and recovery of on-premises VMware VMs or physical Windows/Linux servers to a secondary VMware site using ASR. In a similar way to the physical on-premises infrastructure to Azure scenario, here also we can use ASR for DR as showcased in Figure 2-6.

1. We need to set up the component servers in
    both the primary and secondary physical sites
    (configuration, process, master target) and install
    the Unified Agent on machines that we want to
    replicate and protect.

2. After initial replication, the agent on each machine
    sends delta changes to the process server for
    replication.

3. The process server optimizes the data and transfers
    it to the master target server on the secondary site.
    The configuration server manages the replication
    process.

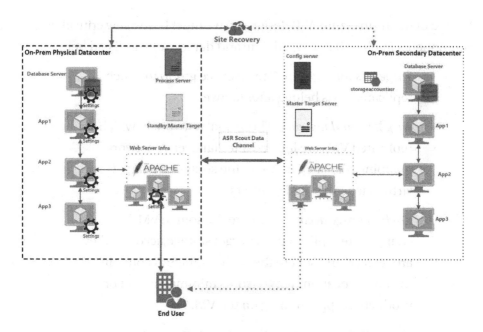

Figure 2-6. *Deprecated physical/VMWare to secondary site*

Major Components, Prerequisites, and Planning and Design Considerations for Each of the ASR Scenarios

Now that we have covered all the different scenarios that can be managed by ASR, let us take a closer look to understand what preplanning is required for each of these scenarios. This is key to have in place before we make design decisions.

We must first understand the architecture components for each of the scenarios we are going to encounter while defining and deploying ASR.

Azure to Azure

In case of Azure-to-Azure ASR designing, we must have a few critical components in place before we define and deploy ASR, as listed here.

- *Target resource group*: The resource group to which replicated VMs belong after failover.

- *Target virtual network*: The virtual network in which replicated VMs are located after failover. A network mapping is created between the source and target virtual networks, and vice versa.

- *Cache storage accounts*: Before the source VMs' changes are replicated to a target storage account, they are tracked and sent to the cache storage account in the target location. This ensures minimal impact on production apps running on the VM.

- *Target storage accounts*: Storage accounts in the target location to which the data is replicated.

- *Target availability sets*: Availability sets in which the replicated VMs are located after failover.

VMware/Physical to Azure Scenario

The following are the architecture components.

- *Azure*: An Azure subscription, Azure storage account, and Azure network. Replicated data from on-premises VMs is stored in the storage account. Azure VMs are created with the replicated data when you run a failover from on-premises to Azure. The Azure VMs connect to the Azure virtual network when they are created.

- *Configuration server*: A single on-premises VMware VM is deployed to run all of the on-premises Site Recovery components. The VM runs the configuration server, process server, and master target server. The configuration server coordinates communications between on-premises and Azure and manages data replication.

- *Process server*: Installed by default together with the configuration server, it acts as a replication gateway. The process server receives replication data; optimizes it with caching, compression, and encryption; and sends it to Azure storage. The process server also installs the Mobility Service on VMs you want to replicate and performs automatic discovery of VMs on on-premises VMware servers. As your deployment grows, you can add additional, separate process servers to handle larger volumes of replication traffic.

- *Master target server*: Installed by default together with the configuration server, the master target server handles replication data during failback from Azure. For large deployments, you can add an additional, separate master target server for failback.

- *VMware servers*: VMware VMs are hosted on on-premises vSphere ESXi servers. We recommend a vCenter server to manage the hosts. During Site Recovery deployment, you add VMware servers to the Recovery Services Vault.

- *Replicated machines*: The Mobility Service is installed on each VMware VM that you replicate. We recommend you allow automatic installation from the process server. Alternatively, you can install the service manually, or use an automated deployment method such as System Center Configuration Manager.

When we are planning for VMware infrastructure DR or migration we must keep the UEFI consideration in mind. Azure does not support VMs running a UEFI/Generation 2 firmware. ASR cannot directly migrate a VM from VMware to Azure IaaS when that VM is using Unified Extensible Firmware Interface (UEFI) firmware, so we have the following options to achieve that.

- *Option 1*: Convert the VMware VM from UEFI to BIOS firmware and use Site Recovery to migrate a BIOS VM from VMware to Azure IaaS.

- *Option 2*: Migrate the VMware VM from UEFI to a Generation 2 Hyper-V VM and use Site Recovery to migrate the VM from the Hyper-V host to Azure IaaS.

- *Option 3*: Use an external vendor tool or manual process that can convert and migrate the VMs between formats in VMware and Azure IaaS.

Hyper-V/VMM to Azure Replication Scenario

The following are the Hyper-V components.

- *Azure*: This requires an Azure subscription, Azure storage account, and Azure network. Replicated data from on-premises VM workloads is stored in the storage account. Azure VMs are created with the replicated workload data when failover from your on-premises site occurs. The Azure VMs connect to the Azure virtual network when they are created.

- *Hyper-V*: During Site Recovery deployment, you gather Hyper-V hosts and clusters into Hyper-V sites. We need to install the ASR Provider and Azure Recovery Services Agent on each Hyper-V machine. The Provider orchestrates replication with ASR over the Internet. The Recovery Services Agent handles data replication. Communications from both the Provider and the Agent are secure and encrypted. Replicated data in Azure storage is also encrypted.

- *Hyper-V VMs*: One or more VMs running on Hyper-V. Nothing needs to be explicitly installed on VMs.

VMM to Azure Requirements

Apart from the architecture components for VMM-based ASR just given, a few additional components are involved.

- *VMM server*: The VMM server has one or more clouds containing Hyper-V hosts. You install the Site Recovery Provider on the VMM server to orchestrate replication with ASR, and register the server in the Recovery Services Vault.

- *Network*: Logical and VM networks are set up on the VMM server. The VM network should be linked to a logical network that is associated with the cloud. VM networks are mapped to Azure virtual networks. When Azure VMs are created after failover, they are added to the Azure network that is mapped to the VM network.

Capacity Planning

When we are going to start planning for DR for any infrastructure, we must perform certain capacity-specific brainstorming, analysis, and consideration before creating the design and deployment. Here are a few points we need to think through in terms of capacity planning.

- Replication (maximum daily change rate)

- Configuration and process server sizing

- Network bandwidth

  - Initial replication

  - Delta replication and peaks

  - Control network bandwidth

- **Storage**

  - Replication

  - Workload IOPS during failovers

  - Test failover (replication and workload IOPS simultaneously)

  - Standard or premium storage

  - Storage account naming convention

- **Computing capacity**

  - Test failovers ensure necessary capacity

We must use ASR Planner for VMware-to-Azure or ASR Planner for Hyper-V-to-Azure, depending on the required scenarios.

Network Considerations and Security

Network Bandwidth

Use Site Recovery Deployment Planner to calculate the bandwidth you need for replication (initial replication and then the delta). This tool will help us to get better metrics in terms of:

- Estimated network bandwidth required for delta replication.

- Throughput that Site Recovery can get from on-premises to Azure.

- Number of VMs to batch, based on the estimated bandwidth to complete the initial replication in each amount of time.

- RPO that can be achieved for a given bandwidth.

- Impact on the desired RPO if lower bandwidth is provisioned.

Control Network Bandwidth

Once we have a better understanding of the bandwidth required, we have a couple of options for controlling the amount of bandwidth that is used for replication.

- VMware traffic that replicates to Azure goes through a specific process server. You can throttle bandwidth on the machines that are running as process servers.

- You can influence the bandwidth that is used for replication by using a couple of registry keys.

  - The `HKEY_LOCAL_MACHINE\SOFTWARE\Microsoft\Windows Azure Backup\Replication\UploadThreadsPerVM` registry value specifies the number of threads that are used for data transfer (initial or delta replication) of a disk. A higher value increases the network bandwidth that is used for replication.

  - The `HKEY_LOCAL_MACHINE\SOFTWARE\Microsoft\Windows Azure Backup\Replication\DownloadThreadsPerVM` registry value specifies the number of threads that are used for data transfer during failback.

Retain IP vs. Change IP

With full subnet failover we should consider retaining IP for a quick scenario reference. Consider a situation where during failover, we might have a requirement that the customer wants to keep the IP addressing in the target region identical to the source region. In an Azure-to-Azure DR scenario for Azure VMs configured with static IP addresses, Site Recovery tries to provision the same IP address for the target VM. In other scenarios we must set network and IP addressing for the target Azure VM to mirror the on-premises setting. Further, we should manage subnets as part of the DR process. We also need an Azure VNet to match the on-premises network, and network routes must be modified to reflect that subnet after failover.

For partial subnet failovers, however, we should consider the change IP approach.

Client Routing

The following are the options for client routing.

- *ASR + Azure Traffic Manager*: This allows you to control the distribution of traffic across your application endpoints.

- *Public IP*: Public IP addresses allow Internet resources to communicate inbound to Azure resources. It also helps us to enable Azure resources to communicate outbound to Internet and public-facing Azure services with an IP address assigned to the resource.

Growth-Factor Consideration: ExpressRoute Circuits

One more key point of consideration is whether or not we required an express route network for our DR infrastructure. This will let us extend our on-premises networks into the Microsoft cloud over a private connection facilitated by a connectivity provider. ASR replicates data to an Azure Storage account or replica managed disk on the target Azure region over a public endpoint. To use ExpressRoute for Site Recovery replication traffic, you can use Microsoft peering or an existing public peering (see Figure 2-7; deprecated for new creations).

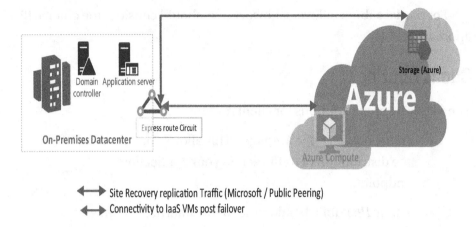

→ Site Recovery replication Traffic (Microsoft / Public Peering)
→ Connectivity to IaaS VMs post failover

Figure 2-7. ExpressRoute circuit

Firewall Rules

Here are some firewall rules to follow so that your ASR configuration can
be successful and replication can be consistent.

- All ASR scenarios require access to the following URLs:

    - `*.hypervrecoverymanager.windowsazure.com`

    - `*.accesscontrol.windows.net`

    - `*.backup.windowsazure.com`

    - `*.blob.core.windows.net`

    - `*.store.core.windows.net`

- All communication happens on https (443).

- IP address-based firewall rules can be created by
  opening up Azure Datacenter IP Ranges for the region
  of Recovery Services Vault and for WUS.

- The IP range can change, therefore it is not recommended to use IP-based firewall rules.

- `ntp://pool.ntp.org` (default port 123, optional).

Security

ASR provides three built-in roles to control Site Recovery management operations.

- *Site Recovery Contributor*: This role has all permissions required to manage ASR operations in a Recovery Services Vault. A user with this role, however, cannot create or delete a Recovery Services Vault or assign access rights to other users. This role is best suited for DR administrators who can enable and manage DR for applications or entire organizations, as the case may be.

- *Site Recovery Operator*: This role has permissions to execute and manage failover and failback operations. A user with this role cannot enable or disable replication, create or delete vaults, register new infrastructure, or assign access rights to other users. This role is best suited for a DR operator who can fail over VMs or applications when instructed by application owners and IT administrators in an actual or simulated disaster situation such as a DR drill. After resolution of the disaster, the DR operator can reprotect and fail back the VMs.

- *Site Recovery Reader*: This role has permissions to view all Site Recovery management operations. This role is best suited for an IT monitoring executive who can monitor the current state of protection and raise support tickets if required.

Some permissions are required to enable replication.

- Permission to create a VM in the selected resource group.

- Permission to create a VM in the selected virtual network.

- Permission to write to the selected Storage account.

You should consider using the Virtual Machine Contributor and Classic Virtual Machine Contributor built-in roles for Resource Manager and Classic deployment models, respectively.

Recovery Plans Consideration

Recovery Plans

Gather machines into recovery groups for the purpose of failover. This helps us to define a systematic recovery process, by creating independent units of an app in our environment that we can fail over.

- Define groups of machines that fail together.

- Model dependencies between machines.

- Automate recovery tasks to reduce RTO.

- Verify that you're prepared for migration or DR by ensuring that your apps are part of a recovery plan.

- Run test failovers on recovery plans, to ensure DR or migration is working as expected.

Customize and Extend Recovery Plans

You can customize and extend recovery plans in several ways.

- *Add new groups*: Add additional recovery plan groups (up to seven) to the default group, and then add more machines or replication groups to those recovery plan groups. Groups are numbered in the order in which you add them. A VM, or replication group, can only be included in one recovery plan group.

- *Add a manual action*: You can add manual actions that run before or after a recovery plan group. When the recovery plan runs, it stops at the point at which you inserted the manual action. A dialog box prompts you to specify that the manual action was completed.

- *Add a script*: You can add scripts that run before or after a recovery plan group. When you add a script, it adds a new set of actions for the group. For example, a set of presteps for Group 1 will be created with the name Group 1: presteps. All presteps will be listed inside this set. You can only add a script on the primary site if you have a VMM server deployed.

- *Add Azure runbooks*: You can extend recovery plans with Azure runbooks; for example, you can use them to automate tasks or to create single-step recovery.

- *Run a failover*: You can run a failover test, planned or unplanned.

Supportability Matrix

Another important consideration we must keep in mind before planning and design take place is the supportability of each scenario. Let's have a closer look at that critical supportability.

Azure-to-Azure Replication Scenario

Here are the operating systems supported for Azure-to-Azure DR.

- Windows platform support

  - Windows Server 2016 (Server Core and Server with Desktop Experience)

  - Windows Server 2012 R2

  - Windows Server 2012

  - Windows Server 2008 R2 with at least Service Pack 1 (SP1)

- Linux platform support

  - Red Hat Enterprise Linux 6.7, 6.8, 6.9, 7.0, 7.1, 7.2, 7.3

  - CentOS 6.5, 6.6, 6.7, 6.8, 6.9, 7.0, 7.1, 7.2, 7.3

  - Ubuntu 14.04 LTS Server

  - Ubuntu 16.04 LTS Server

  - Oracle Enterprise Linux 6.4, 6.5 running either the Red Hat compatible kernel or Unbreakable Enterprise Kernel Release 3 (UEK3)

  - SUSE Linux Enterprise Server 11 Service Pack 3 (SP3)

  - SUSE Linux Enterprise Server 11 Service Pack 4 (SP4)

Here are the computer configuration support settings for Azure-to-Azure DR.

- *Supported*: Any size VM with at least two CPU cores and 1 GB RAM, availability sets, Hybrid Use Benefit (HUB) VMs, Azure Gallery Images (Microsoft and third party), custom images

- *Not supported*: VM scale sets.

Here are the storage configuration support settings for Azure-to-Azure DR.

- *Supported*: Operating system/data disk size, 1023 GB; number of data disks, 64; standard and premium storage accounts; storage spaces, encryption at rest (SSE); locally redundant storage (LRS); geographically redundant storage (GRS); read-access geographically redundant storage (RA-GRS).

- *Not supported*: Temporary disk, standard or premium managed disks, Azure Disk, Encryption, hot add/remove disk, zone redundant storage, cool and hot storage.

Tables 2-1 and 2-2 show the supported and unsupported network configuration support settings, respectively.

Table 2-1. *Network Configuration Support for Azure-to-Azure Disaster Recovery*

Configuration	Remarks
Network interface (NIC), up to maximum number of NICs supported by a specific Azure VM size	NICs are created when the VM is created as part of test failover or failover operation. The number of NICs on the failover VM depends on the number of NICs the source VM has at the time of enabling replication. If you add or remove a NIC after enabling replication, it does not impact the NIC count on the failover VM.
Internet and internal load balancer	You need to associate the preconfigured load balancer using an Azure automation script in a recovery plan.
Public IP	You need to associate an already existing public IP to the NIC or create one and associate it to the NIC using an Azure automation script in a recovery plan.
NSG on NIC (Resource Manager)	You need to associate the NSG to the NIC using an Azure automation script in a recovery plan.
NSG on subnet (Resource Manager and Classic)	You need to associate the NSG to the NIC using an Azure automation script in a recovery plan.
Reserved IP (Static IP)/ Retain source IP	If the NIC on the source VM has static IP configuration and the target subnet has the same IP available, it is assigned to the failover VM. If the target subnet does not have the same IP available, one of the available IPs in the subnet is reserved for this VM. You can specify a fixed IP of your choice in Replicated Item ➤ Settings ➤ Compute and Network ➤ Network Interfaces. You can select the NIC and specify the subnet and IP of your choice.

(continued)

Table 2-1. (*continued*)

Configuration	Remarks
Dynamic IP	If the NIC on the source VM has dynamic IP configuration, the NIC on the failover VM is also dynamic by default. You can specify a fixed IP of your choice in Replicated Item ➤ Settings ➤ Compute and Network ➤ Network Interfaces. You can select the NIC and specify the subnet and IP of your choice.
Traffic Manager integration	You can preconfigure your Traffic Manager in such a way that the traffic is routed to the endpoint in the source region on a regular basis and to the endpoint in the target region in case of failover.
Site-to-Site VPN with on-premises (with or without ExpressRoute)	Ensure that the UDRs and NSGs are configured in such a way that the Site Recovery traffic is not routed to on-premises.
Azure-managed DNS	An effective and efficient solution to divert network traffic uses a DNS-based failover mechanism using Azure DNS (authoritative DNS). Azure DNS works best when used in conjunction with a cold standby DR approach.
Unauthenticated Proxy	Azure Site Recovery Mobility Service agent did not autodetect the proxy settings and does not support the authenticated proxies scenario. Also make sure all the required URL and required IP ranges are allowed.
VNET-to-VNET connection	VNet-to-VNet communication can be combined with multisite configurations that will establish network topologies that combine cross-premises connectivity with intervirtual network connectivity.

Table 2-2. *Network Configuration Not Supported for Azure-to-Azure Disaster Recovery*

Configuration	Remarks
Authenticated proxy	If the VM is using an authenticated proxy for outbound connectivity, it cannot be replicated using ASR.

VMware/Physical to Azure Scenario

Here are the operating systems that support VMware/physical to Azure DR.

- Windows platform supports

  - Windows Server 2019

  - Windows Server 2016 64-bit

  - Windows Server 2012 R2

  - Windows Server 2012

  - Windows Server 2008 R2 with at least SP1

  - Windows 10, Windows 8.1, Windows 8, and Windows 7 with SP1 64-bit clients

- Linux platform supports

  - Red Hat Enterprise Linux 5.2 to 5.11, 6.1 to 6.9, 7.0 to 8.1

  - CentOS 5.2 to 5.11, 6.1 to 6.10, 7.0 to 7.6, 8.0 to 8.1

  - Ubuntu 14.04 LTS Server, Ubuntu 16.04 LTS Server and Ubuntu 18.04 LTS server

  - Oracle Enterprise Linux 6.4, 6.5, 6.6, 6.7, 6.8, 6.9, 6.10, 7.0, 7.1, 7.2, 7.3, 7.4, 7.5, 7.6, 7.7

- SUSE Linux Enterprise Server 11 SP3, SUSE Linux Enterprise Server 11 SP4, Server 12 SP1, SP2, SP3, SP4, Server 15, 15 SP1

- Debian 7, 8

Here are the computer configuration support settings for VMware/physical to Azure DR.

- *Supported*: Availability sets, HUB, managed disks.

- *Not supported*: Fail back to on-premises from Azure VM with managed disks

Here are the storage configuration support settings for VMware/physical to Azure DR.

- *Host storage supported*: Network File System (NFS), Storage Area Network (SAN) (ISCSI), multipath (MPIO).

- *Guest storage supported*: Virtual Machine Disk (VMDK), Raw Device Mapping (RDM), disk > 1 TB, disk with 4K sector size, volume with striped disk > 1 TB, exclude disk.

- *Guest storage not supported*: EFI/UEFI, shared cluster disk, encrypted disk, NFS, SMB 3.0, storage spaces, hot add/remove disk.

- *Azure storage supported*: LRS, GRS, RA-GRS, SSE, premium storage.

- *Azure storage not supported*: Cool storage, hot storage, import/export service.

The following are the network configuration support settings for VMware/physical to Azure DR.

- *Host network supported*: NIC Teaming, VLAN, IPv4.

- *Host network not supported*: IPv6.

- *Guest network supported*: IPv4, Static IP, multi-NIC.

- *Guest network not supported*: NIC Teaming, IPv6.

Hyper-V/VMM to Azure Replication Scenario

The operating system supportability settings for Hyper-V both with and without SCVMM to Azure DR include any guest operating system supported by Azure.

Here are the computing configuration support settings for Hyper-V both with and without SCVMM to Azure DR.

- *Supported*: Availability sets, HUB, managed disks.

These are the storage configuration support settings for Hyper-V both with and without SCVMM to Azure DR.

- *Host storage*: SMB 3.0, SAN (ISCSI), Multipath (MPIO).

- *Guest storage supported*: VHD/VHDX, Gen 2 VM, EFI/ UEFI, disk > 1 TB, disk with 4K sector size, volume with striped disk > 1 TB, exclude disk, storage spaces, MPIO.

- *Guest storage not supported*: Shared cluster disk, encrypted disk, SMB 3.0, hot add/remove disk.

- *Azure storage supported*: LRS, GRS, RA-GRS, SSE, premium storage.

- *Azure storage not supported*: Cool storage, hot storage, import/export service.

Here are the network configuration support settings for Hyper-V both with and without SCVMM to Azure DR.

- *Host network supported*: NIC Teaming, VLAN, IPv4.

- *Host network not supported*: IPv6.

- *Guest network supported*: IPv4, Static IP (Windows), Multi-NIC.

- *Guest network not supported*: Static IP (Linux), NIC Teaming, IPv6.

Summary

In this chapter we discussed and explored the challenges we had in the conventional datacenter era and what benefits ASR has introduced. We also looked at the key supported scenarios for ASR, defining and decision planning, and designing and developing a good recovery plan using ASR.

We have discussed the major architecture components that are required before decision making and during planning. The intention is to consider all possible critical decision-making points before we designing the DR configuration.

We also discussed how to check all possible core requirements and the critical supportability matrix to better plan a strong DR infrastructure. We also explored ASR service capabilities to address different scenarios. As we move to the next chapters, we will take deep dive into different scenarios, tools, capabilities, and design points and learn more with scenario-based examples.

CHAPTER 3

Recovering Microsoft Azure Workloads to Another Azure Region

We have discussed Microsoft Azure's platform capabilities to provide resiliency in previous chapters. We discussed storage, networks, VMs, and other services that are built from the ground up with capabilities to support various kinds of failures. Although applications deployed on Azure leveraging such services can benefit from their resiliency, they will not necessarily have default DR capabilities aligned to your RPO and RTO requirements.

Microsoft Azure is the first cloud service provider to offer DR capabilities for its IaaS workloads as a native feature. This is achieved by replicating the VM to another region, making your applications resilient to even an entire region failure. With this, one can design infrastructure against hardware-level failures (with availability set), datacenter-level failures (with availability zones), and regional failures (with regional pairs). By choosing Azure as a DR solution, enterprises reap several benefits.

© Bapi Chakraborty and Yashajeet Chowdhury 2020
B. Chakraborty and Y. Chowdhury, *Introducing Disaster Recovery with Microsoft Azure*,
https://doi.org/10.1007/978-1-4842-5917-7_3

- *DR as a service:* With ASR as a service offering,
  you can enable replication of IaaS workloads to
  a different Azure region within a geographical
  cluster without having to provision additional
  infrastructure and software procurement. Because
  this is a service, you get 99.9% SLA, 24/7 support for
  the service, replication monitoring, and continuous
  updates. This eliminates a lot of management and
  administrative overhead.

- *Automatic resource creation:* The entire process
  of creating a DR region involves many additional
  activities beyond just resource creation and
  deployment. ASR makes the entire process seamless
  and simple by creating storage and a network
  automatically and by providing capabilities for
  integrating with database services such as SQL
  databases and SQL AlwaysOn availability groups as
  part of the recovery plan.

- *Test failover and DR drills:* ASR enables you to test the
  DR process, set the order of resource creation, and test
  those resource to ensure there aren't any surprises
  when it comes to recovering from a catastrophe.
  Traditionally, a lot of effort, coordination, planning,
  and outages were involved in executing an end-to-end
  DR drill. With ASR, it is much easier to run such DR
  drills without affecting current production workloads
  or replication. This in turn increases your confidence in
  your DR solution, ensuring it will work when you need
  it the most.

- *Recovery plan:* With recovery plans you can define a single unit of failure and how you wish to recovery your workload. For example, you need to bring up the databases before you bring the application servers or front-end web servers online and ensure that they are consistent.

- *Optimization and continuous updates:* By adopting ASR and its capabilities, you are assured that you continue to receive feature and security updates when they are available without having to take care of them. Also, it provides for advanced compression capabilities to reduce network bandwidth utilization.

It is important to understand, however, that in certain scenarios, ASR will not be able to provide the entire solution for recovery, and additional tools and scripts might need to be used for automated recovery. This is specifically for scenarios wherein both IaaS and PaaS solutions are used together. With these in mind, let us now discuss the following topics in this chapter.

- Azure-to-Azure architectures.

- Supportability of ASR for various workloads.

- Design considerations for an Azure-to-Azure scenario.

- Sample scenarios with Infrastructure-as-a-Service (IaaS) and Platform-as-a-Service (PaaS) deployments.

Azure-to-Azure Architecture

For Azure VMs, to be able to create a replica and recover in one of the target regions, we need to keep in mind that the source and target regions are within the same geographic clusters. For example, there are several regions that are part of the geographic cluster Asia: South India,

Central India, West India, Southeast Asia, East Asia, Japan East, Japan West, Korea Central, Korea South, UAE Central, and UAE North. Do not confuse this with the concept of a regional pair, whereby each region has a corresponding regional pair. Two very important points should be kept in mind.

- Availability of the source VM size in the target region.

- If there are other services such as Application Gateway, SQL databases, load balancers, or app services in use in the entire application in the source region and availability and planning of each of them in the target region.

Tables 3-1 through 3-3 depict a broader set of components in use while configuring DR of a VM using the portal.

Table 3-1. Source Components

Source VMs	This can be one or more VM in an availability set in the source region, in this case Southeast Asia.
VM disks	These are the storage disks attached to a VM; the disks can be managed or unmanaged.
Virtual network	The source network and its related network security groups.
Cache storage account	This is the location where all data is cached before replicating to the target location during replication.

Table 3-2. *Target Components*

Target VMs	These VMs will be created when a failover is performed.
VM disks	These are the storage disks attached to a VM; the disks can be managed or unmanaged and created once a failover is performed.
Virtual network	The target virtual network. The once a failover is performed, ASR will create the virtual network. It is possible, however, to precreate this and configure the VMs to be connected to the specific network as well. Network security groups and any other routing configurations might have to be configured separately based on specific requirements.
Storage account	This is the location where all data is replicated if the source disks are on an unmanaged storage account. A corresponding managed disk is created where the VM disks use managed storage. These settings are managed by Site Recovery Services.
Site Recovery Service	Might be hosted in the target region or another region in the same geo.
Automation account	An automation account is also created to support automatic updates of the VM extension or mobility agent that helps to replicate the VM. Only one such automation account is created per subscription.
Availability set or Availability zones	ASR also creates a corresponding availability set or zone based on the source environment configuration. ASR autodetects source availability sets and assigns the same to the recovered VMs.

Table 3-3. *Other Components*

Replication policy	ASR creates a replication policy to specify how long it keeps each recovery point and how often to take application-consistent snapshots. You can precreate them and reuse them while enabling replication of a VM.
Snapshots and recovery points	ASR creates recovery points from a point-in-time snapshot of the VMs' state. ASR takes a crash-consistent snapshot by default and captures further application-consistent snapshots based on the frequency specified in the configuration. Crash-consistent snapshots are taken every five minutes and cannot be modified.

Replication Overview

Figure 3-1 depicts a sample VM replication from the Southeast Asia region to the South India region and includes the components previously mentioned.

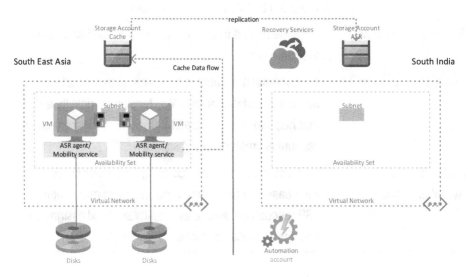

Figure 3-1. *Azure-to-Azure VM replication components*

The Replication Process

Replication can be enabled for a VM from within the Azure portal under the Operations settings. The following things happen once you enable replication.

1. The Site Recovery Agent or the Mobility agent extension is provisioned into the source VM. This is an automated process.

2. The VM is registered into the Recovery Services Vault.

3. Replication begins and all writes are stored into the cache storage at the source site.

4. ASR processes the data and replicates it to the target site storage account.

5. Once the data is processed, appropriate restore points are created at specified intervals.

6. If automatic update of the recovery extension is configured, an automation account is created per subscription and a job is configured.

7. For authentication purposes, an Azure Active Directory RunAs account is also created and configured with certificate authentication.

Figure 3-2 depicts the set of jobs executed once replication was enabled for a VM named VM002 using the Azure portal.

Site Recovery jobs
vault218

∇ Filter   Export jobs

Name	↑↓	Status	↑↓	Type	↑↓	Item	↑↓	Start...↑↓	Duration
Finalize protection on the recovery virtual machine		⊘ Successful		Protected item		vm002		2/15/202...	00:00:02
Finalize protection on the primary virtual machine		⊘ Successful		Protected item		vm002		2/15/202...	00:00:00
Protection configuration		⊘ Successful		Cloud		asr-a2a-default-southeastasia-container		2/15/202...	00:00:04
Protection configuration		⊘ Successful		Cloud		asr-a2a-default-southindia-container		2/15/202...	00:00:07
Enable replication		⊘ Successful		Protected item		vm002		2/15/202...	00:07:39
Associate replication policy		⊘ Successful		Replication policy		24-hour-retention-policy		2/15/202...	00:01:07
Map Networks		⊘ Successful		Network		vn-sea-asr		2/15/202...	00:00:01
Associate replication policy		⊘ Successful		Replication policy		24-hour-retention-policy		2/15/202...	00:01:06
Create protection container		⊘ Successful		Cloud		asr-a2a-default-southindia-container		2/15/202...	00:00:00
Map Networks		⊘ Successful		Network		vn-sea		2/15/202...	00:00:02
Create a site		⊘ Successful		Server		asr-a2a-default-southindia		2/15/202...	00:01:07
Create protection container		⊘ Successful		Cloud		asr-a2a-default-southeastasia-container		2/15/202...	00:00:00
Create a site		⊘ Successful		Server		asr-a2a-default-southeastasia		2/15/202...	00:01:05
Create replication policy		⊘ Successful		Replication policy		24-hour-retention-policy		2/15/202...	00:00:00

Figure 3-2. *ASR jobs and status once replication is enabled*

Once the initial replication is completed, you can visualize the replication settings and its geographical representation. Figure 3-3 is a plotting of replication source and target after replication was enabled for the virtual machine VM002 from Southeast Asia to South India.

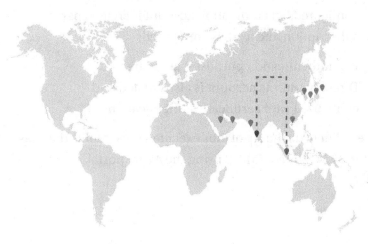

Figure 3-3. *VM VM002 being replicated from Southeast Asia to South India*

What we have discussed so far is mostly in the case of a simple VM-based DR configuration capability. This is just to show how ASR works while enabled for IaaS-based workloads. We all know this will not be the scenario for most applications. There will be multiple VMs with a combination of multiple PaaS services and complex interdependencies with internal and external integration. Before we dive deeper into complex, real-world scenarios, let us quickly look into the various supportability matrix requirements.

Design Considerations

In planning and designing a DR solution with ASR, constraints and limitations of the tools, platform capabilities, cost-effectiveness of the solution, and various supportability factors should be carefully considered. Although there are some common considerations across any scenario, the context and source solution might change when we consider the target design. For example, tools, scripts, and processes for an on-premises system and a cloud-based system might be different. The sections that follow detail some of the broader considerations.

RPO and RTO Requirements

One of the primary deciding factors of the entire DR method includes establishing the RTO and RPO. This is a common factor across all scenarios, for both the source and target location. How quickly you want your systems back and what amount of data loss you can sustain determines the type of DR required—hot, cold, or warm. We discussed this in detail in Chapter 1. For Azure workloads, we need to consider the source and target region, services availability, whether to design a like-to-like environment, or a minimalistic deployment that can be scaled up as required. The greatest benefit we get on Azure is the platform capability to replicate a heavy workload and a large volume of data. We explore a few such scenarios in upcoming sections in this chapter.

Nonfunctional Requirements

Clarity in terms of nonfunctional requirements (NFRs) and objectives
helps to create the end-to-end design of the DR solution. NFRs typically
include performance, availability, scalability, capacity, reliability, data
integrity, regulatory, interoperability, security, and maintenance of the
solution. These requirements also help decide how the target solution
has to be designed. For example, a capacity NFR might decide if the target
system must be provisioned with minimal sizing to ensure only a selective
user location is to be serviced during the outage window. A maintainability
NFR might require failback planning and protection of the target DR
system within a specific period of time postoutage.

Region, Subscription, and Resource Group

Choice of a region for developing, designing, and deploying a DR
solution is one of the first important considerations. Each Azure region
is configured as a paired region for another region. When Azure releases
updates or plans for maintenance, it serializes across its paired regions
so that both regions in the same pair are not affected. Also, in the event
of an entire regional disaster, at least one location in each regional pair
is prioritized for recovery, ensuring the highest possible availability at
the platform level. Similarly, storage accounts and several other services
can leverage such regional pairs to replicate and recover workloads
in the event of a disaster when the primary region is not available.
Visit https://docs.microsoft.com/en-us/azure/best-practices-
availability-paired-regions for a detailed description of regional
pairs and how they help with an effective DR design.

Second, you need to plan whether both production and DR resources
should exist in the same or different subscriptions. For mission-critical
workloads where there are several applications made up of hundreds of
systems, organizations prefer to go for a separate subscription. This not

only provides isolation, but also helps achieve additional scalability and manageability. See Azure subscriptions and limits for more details at `https://docs.microsoft.com/en-us/azure/azure-resource-manager/ management/azure-subscription-service-limits`.

A resource group is a collection of resources from the same or different regions that share the same life cycle. There can be various constructs based on which resource group is planned for your DR solution. Typically, it is of the same as your source Azure deployment in the target region. However, in certain cases, where DR design includes deploying applications and data in multiple regions and each region is scaled to handle the traffic or user load in the event one of the other regions fails, resource groups should be planned in such a way that common resources that are leveraged by more than one region can be put together in a separate resource group (e.g., Traffic Manager and CDN services). Because these are global and can be designed as common resources across multiple regions, combining them in another resource group can increase the availability of your application.

Networking

Networking is one of the most critical components to design for a DR scenario. In designing an Azure-to-Azure DR scenario, networking components and choice of the underlying network heavily depends on the design of the application and what specific DR scenarios are you trying to address. Is it only a component-level failure, service-level failure, protection against a datacenter-level failure, or an entire region outage? Depending on which scenario is your priority and your RTO and RPO requirements, the choice of the network and its DR components will vary. For example, for a two-tier single node, each IaaS-based application, with Web front and database servers, having them deployed in an availability zone will protect against a single datacenter failure. Hence networking components such as a putting two web front ends behind a standard load balancer and leveraging application-based DR capability for a database such as a SQL Server AlwaysOn availability group with two nodes spread across two availability zones would suffice. The same design will not help if there is a regional failure, though, so we need to choose another region with a different virtual network with additional network connectivity from on-premises, source virtual network, and automation scripts to perform postrecovery activities. Broadly, consider the following factors while designing the network.

- What is the current networking design and layout? This includes the current and source Azure networking design model: Is it hub and spoke, mesh, or flat architecture? Are multiple subnets, specific IP addressing, and cross-region connectivity, including on-premises?

- How is the application or server accessed and from where?

- What inbound and outbound connectivity requirements should be considered?

- Is there any firewall or network virtual appliance in use? Do they need to be available in the target region, too?

- Various URLs and IP addresses should be whitelisted for ASR or other tools for replicating the source environment.

- Will you recover within the same subscription or in a different subscription? How will the hybrid network connectivity across on-premises, Azure, and over the internet be handled?

- Will other networking components such as network security groups, firewalls, WAFs, load balancers, Traffic Manager, application gateway for multiregional deployments be precreated or created at the time of recovery?

- How long does it take to deploy these components and how does it affect the overall RTO?

- What postprovisioning activities will be required and how they will be handled? Manually or in an automated process?

- Will all application dependencies exist in the source region or are some hosted on-premises as well? If that is the case, will we need to create an additional ExpressRoute connection to the DR region as well?

- Consider using virtual network service endpoints for storage if the source deployment uses a custom route to divert Internet-bound traffic (0.0.0.0/0 address prefix) to on-premises network appliances.

- Where NSGs are in use for controlling outbound traffic, consider using service tags for Storage, EventHub, AzureAD, and AzureSiteRecovery in your NSG, and test them before applying to the production environment.

Figure 3-4 depicts a sample blueprint of very high-level network connectivity with an on-premises integration requirement. Note that the target Azure region exists on a different subscription to protect against a security compromise scenario of the source subscription.

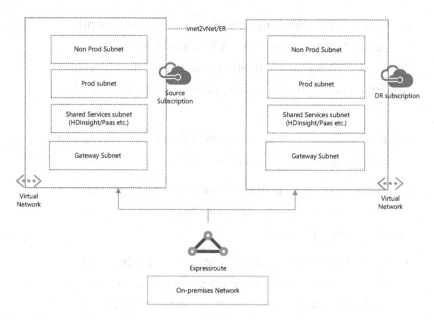

Figure 3-4. *Network layout with hybrid connectivity with on-premises*

Computing

The target design for DR depends heavily on what computing service you use for your source Azure application. For example, considerations for tools usage and recovery steps will be different based on whether computing service is a VM, batch service, app service plan, Kubernetes cluster, or a VM scale set. If your computer is a VM, you should consider using ASR. ASR supports all major versions of Windows and Linux. Other associated resources of a VM, such as storage, network interface, and so on, should also be considered. Some important factors for a VM are as follows.

- Windows Server 2008 R2 with SP1/SP2 and newer versions of Windows Server operating systems are supported. However, for Windows Server 2008 R2, you need to install the SHA-2 update to support the ASR Mobility agent.

- Windows 7 (x64) SP1 with SHA-2 update with supported Mobility agent version, and higher Windows Client operating systems are supported.

- All major Linux distributions including Red Hat Enterprise Linux, CentOS, Ubuntu, Debian, SUSE Linux Enterprise Server, and Oracle Linux versions are supported. As for file systems, ASR supports ext3, ext4, XFS, BTRFS, ReiserFS (SUSE Linux Enterprise Server only), LVM2 volume manager, and Device Mapper multipath software.

- For details on every kernel version, please check the Microsoft online documentation for an updated information. It is possible that by the time of the release of the book certain supportabilities are changed.

- VM scale sets are not yet supported with ASR, so separate considerations such as rapid deployment a using DevOps pipeline with infrastructure as code and with application deployment is a suitable option.

- Role-Based Access Control (RBAC) and VM extensions are not replicated as part of VM replication. A manual or automated task needs to be planned to create necessary RBAC and provision the VM extensions.

- Consider availability of appropriate VM sizes in the target DR region.

- Resizing the VM disk before failover is advisable. If you change after failover such changes aren't captured by ASR. Addition of a new disk to a replicated VM is supported.

- If you have customized operating system disks, please consider that operating system disk maximum size is 2048 GB, 8192 for managed disks, and 4095 for unmanaged disks. The maximum number of disks per VM is 64 as per Azure supportability. Maximum disk change rate should be no more than 10 MBps per premium disk and 2 MBps per standard disk. Replication might not be able to keep up with the change rates if the change rates are consistently higher.

- Consider using automation scripts for certain postprovisioning tasks in the target DR region, such as configuration and association of a load balancer, public IP address, and NSG to a network card or subnet.

Based on our previous application model in Figure 3-1, Figure 3-5 displays a hybrid connectivity requirement from on-premises. The application is a single web and database server, each deployed in an IaaS model in two different subnets in a virtual network. We need to protect it against regional failure, but there is no need for HA. We have two options here. We can back up both the systems using Azure backup service and redeploy and restore in the target region. Second, we can enable recovery extension for these VMs and recover them in another region in the event of a disaster. Should we have multiple applications and deployments and users need to access them from on-premises, connectivity with dedicated ExpressRoute will be the best possible solution. This requires further information gathering before deciding on the final model because it involves increased cost.

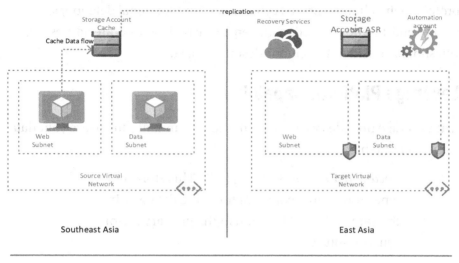

On-premises

Figure 3-5. *Sample disaster recovery design with ASR and with hybrid connectivity*

It is evident that several factors and requirements influence what networking layout and components are chosen. It is advisable to refer to the latest online documentation before planning any DR solution because some of the capabilities or supportability matrix might change from time to time.

Storage

There are two aspects for Microsoft Azure storage accounts to protect against failures and to keep your application data safe. On one hand, you want to ensure that data is available and protected against hardware, datacenter, zonal, and regional failure; on the other hand you also need to protect against human errors, cyberattack, unintentional deletion, and so on. For end-to-end protection and ensuring both aspects are addressed, you should consider the options described next.

Leverage Platform Capability

Azure storage provides various options for redundancy to ensure your data is always available.

- *Locally redundant storage (LRS):* This storage type stores three copies of the same data within the same physical location in the primary region synchronously.

- *Zone-redundant storage (ZRS):* Data is stored synchronously across three Azure availability zones within the primary region. This option protects against a single datacenter failure and provides data HA.

- *Geo-redundant storage (GRS):* In this case, data is stored three times synchronously in the same physical location and then copied asynchronously to a secondary region. This choice helps to keep your data and application protected against regional failures. Should you require a read-only endpoint of the asynchronous copy in the secondary region (paired region), you can choose read-access geo-redundant storage. This choice is useful when the primary region is down and Microsoft still did not initiate a failover. You can still access your data without any write functionality and continue to run your application in a possible reduced functionality mode.

- *Geo-zone-redundant storage(G-ZRS):* With G-ZRS you can keep three copies of your data across thee availability zones and have it copied asynchronously to a secondary region. This will provide the highest availability and redundancy. For read-only access in the secondary region, you can also enable read access. This type is known as RA-G-ZRS.

Although we have several options for redundancy, there is always a lag for asynchronous copy of the data in the secondary region. Hence, in the event of a failure in the primary region, the ongoing transactions and certain data might not be available in the secondary region because it was never committed or replicated.

Backup

In addition to choosing the appropriate tier for redundancy and planning a storage account as part of the DR solution, a backup plan should also be considered for the critical data you own. The preceding options will ensure you always have accessed to your data somewhere in the event of an unexpected failure, but they do not protect against accidental deletion or error, data corruption, cyberattacks, ransomware attacks, and so on. Hence, a backup and restore strategy should also be included as part of your recovery solution. We can create a custom backup process or use an existing third-party tool. For block blobs, consider taking block blob snapshots and storing them in another storage account in another region. You can use AzCopy or Azure PowerShell to copy to another storage account. Similarly, for file shares, you can use share snapshots. In a recent development, Azure Backup now supports Azure file shares, too. AzCopy can be used to export the contents of a data table to another storage account in another region.

Replicated Machine Storage Consideration

ASR has certain design specifications in terms of what it can support for
the replicated machines. The following items are some of the important
support matrix items for VM disks.

- Maximum operating system disk size is 2048 GB.

- Temporary disks are not replicated. Hence, do not store
  anything on the D: drive (temporary disk).

- The maximum number of disks is 64. Look to
  consolidate disks if the limits are met.

- For storage accounts only LRS and GRS types
  are supported. ZRS types of storage accounts are
  unsupported.

- Azure Disk Encryption on unmanaged disks is not
  supported.

- Maximum size for a data disk is 8192 GB for managed
  disks and 4095 GB for unmanaged disks.

- Also consider the recovery region so that it is aligned
  to the storage account replication and VM replication
  region. Paired region consideration is essential to avoid
  rework of the recovery solution at a later time.

Internal and External Dependencies

This is a common factor for all applications under consideration for
DR. We need to be extra careful about the Azure-to-Azure scenario
if there are any on-premises dependencies or integration in place.
For example, if the application on Azure sends emails from an on-
premises Simple Mail Transfer Protocol (SMTP) server and functional

requirements remain the same, email functionality should continue to be available from the DR solution as well. In that case, careful firewall exclusions, network routing, and integration must happen from the DR network as well. Similar efforts will be required for identity systems as well. For example, for any application that depends on Active Directory and requires integration, the Active Directory infrastructure should either be present in the DR site or a plan has be set out to address such critical prerequisites.

Process and Responsibilities

The end-to-end process and responsibility matrix should be established for DR and post-DR activities. You will have to coordinate and collaborate across various teams naming networking, application storage, database, testing, end users, and so on, during and after the failover. Who from each respective organization or department will be available and what function that person or team will own should be discussed, detailed, established, and clearly documented. You cannot be expected to identify these actors in the middle of a recovery process. Most large and established organizations already have an established DR process and contacts identified for each protected system. However, this might not be the case for all who are new to the cloud, migrating to the cloud, and still adopting it. Hence, it is worth mentioning this consideration to be evaluated and addressed properly during DR design. Once the process and responsibilities are established, consider an end-to-end failover test to identify and remediate any gaps.

Failback Decisions

Failback decisions typically include how long to continue to operate from the DR or secondary location even though primary region is available. Do you want to fail back your application to the primary location? Will this affect any other additional design and configuration considerations if all functionality is required to be available from the DR site and for the duration of the DR site to remain active? Such decisions could affect further IT processes and actions.

Services in Use on Azure

While building a DR plan on Azure, the more we understand each service and its dependencies, the better the predictability of the solution. Similarly, using the built-in capabilities of the Azure services can provide enhanced resiliency. The capabilities for each service will be different and how you can recover will be different, too. For an Azure-to-Azure DR scenario, where an application might use multiple Azure-based services, you need to carefully ascertain each service before finalizing the recovery process. Let us look at some of the Azure services and the considerations to recover them in another region. Remember, most managed (PaaS) services on Azure have inherent HA capability in the primary region. The details shown in Table 3-4 pertain to ARM deployments only; for updated information, please visit the Azure documentation for each service.

Table 3-4. *Azure Services and Considerations*

Service Name	Considerations
Azure Virtual Network	For most scenarios, precreating the target region virtual network with all necessary subnets is necessary with appropriate IP address ranges to be able to create a warm, cold, or hot/active DR solution. At the time of DR, you do not want to figure out which IP segments to use, what routing and firewall ports should be open, how the gateways should be configured, what the subnets should look like, and so on. This becomes of utmost importance to ensure all secondary region deployments of networking components are chalked out to the greatest detail when on-premises integration exists with a site-to-site VPN or with ExpressRoute connectivity. This is because you cannot connect two similar IP segments to the on-premises network. In certain scenarios, a less proactive approach to precreating the virtual network might exist. When that happens, we can do the following. • Export the virtual network configuration template, and store it in a storage account to create the network from scratch if required with similar settings and configurations. • Use a PowerShell script to re-create the virtual network and all other deployment components that are required to recover the production environment. *(continued)*

Table 3-4. (*continued*)

Service Name	Considerations
Azure App Service	The site contents and the application code will be stateless for App services to be leveraged. In an event involving only application instance or App service outages, a new app instance can be deployed, and you can download and publish the latest backup of the application site content. Similarly, if the latest copy of the site content or application code is available, the same can be deployed to an alternate location to recover from a datacenter or regional failure. Alternatively, when advanced DevOps practices are adopted, the most recent copy of the code can be pushed to an alternate region's App service environment or App service. Of course, all appropriate networking, setup, and configuration with respect to accessibility and routing and deployment prerequisites has to happen to embrace such a DR solution.
SQL Database	SQL Database service is built on a highly resilient platform that guarantees automatic recovery and a minimum of 99.99% SLA against hardware or software failures. In addition, there are a host of various features that enable an architect to design for all possible scenarios. Here are a few such capabilities to consider: • *Temporal tables and deleted databases:* You can maintain full version history of data changes without requiring any custom coding. You can recover from specific row versions if required to support application or human errors. Similarly, the service allows for restoration of a deleted database in the same SQL Server instance.

- *Automated backups and point-in-time restore:* You can recover the entire database based on a configured retention period (up to 35 days). SQL databases keep automatic backups and enable you to restore from them. The backups are stored in an RA-GRS storage account and the service support point-in-time restore from the backup. It captures a full backup weekly, a differential backup every 12 hours, and a transactional log backup every five to ten minutes.

- *Long-term retention:* You can store long-term backups up to ten years for regulation and compliance purposes. You can create necessary policies from within the Azure portal, Azure PowerShell.

- *Active geo-replication:* With active geo-replication you can create up to four replicas in the same server or a different server in another region. The replicas can be readable and require manual effort to perform failover. Azure Managed Instances do not support this feature. It is also possible to create active geo-replication across resources in a different subscription. In the event of a disaster, application data can be brought online in another region once the replica is marked as primary.

- *Auto failover group:* Auto failover group enables automatic detection of failure and recovery of a group of SQL databases in another server region.

HDInsight   HDInsight leverages Azure blob storage. The Hadoop cluster runs its jobs against this data and must be in the same location as the storage account. The best method is to use geo-replicated storage accounts and at the time of disaster, we can redeploy the Hadoop cluster in the paired region.

(continued)

Table 3-4. (*continued*)

Service Name	Considerations
Azure Load Balancer	Azure load balancers require you to deploy the instances in another region to be able to recover the application. Hence, Azure Load Balancer can be provisioned as part of the infrastructure as code CI/CD process in the case of passive recovery scenarios. As for active-active and warm DR, the Azure Load Balancers should be preprovisioned to ensure shorter recovery time. While planning for load balancers, remember that basic load balancers do not support availability zones.
Azure Database for PostgreSQL	Azure database for PostgreSQL primarily enables *point-in-time* restores from backup and *geo-restore* from geo-replicated backups.
	• Point-in-time restore helps to protect against human error or application corruption. This includes restoring an original server or to a new server.
	• In the case of a datacenter-wide outage you could possibly wait or restore to a new instance in another region. Geo-restore uses geo-redundant backup storage in a paired region to maintain, store, and restore in the event the primary region is unavailable.
	• If you have a multiregional deployment, you can leverage cross regional read replicas. The replication is asynchronous and can design multiregional availability and recovery.

Azure Database for MySQL	Inline with Azure Database for PostgreSQL, Azure Database for MySQL also enables similar capabilities. It supports both point-in-time restore from a backup, geo-restore, and read replicas. You can create up to five read replicas from the master, and this uses asynchronous replication. Cross-region replication is a useful method to plan for recovery in another region. This is equivalent to creating new servers and enabling read replication for the database.
Azure Cloud Services	If you are using Azure Cloud Services with web roles, worker roles from the traditional classic model, you can choose either of the following patterns for sustaining regional failures.
	• If the application is not critical, and you can wait for the primary site recovery, you can possibly wait until Azure services are recovered.
	• Deploy your application to an alternate region, ensure data is replicated, and enable application connectivity. This might not be a very suitable option when strict RTO requirements need to be met.
	• Multiple or multiregional deployments with Traffic Manager are used for global load balancing. This model helps when an entire region experiences an outage and the application can serve users from another region. The deployment modes could be active-active or active-standby based on the SLA or RTO requirements.

(continued)

107

Table 3-4. (*continued*)

Service Name	Considerations
Cosmos DB	You can create a Cosmos account, which is distributed across n number of Azure regions. With this you will have at least four copies of data for each region. Hence Cosmos DB enables low latency with high availability of your data.
	Based on your application design and global deployment pattern, you can choose to have the number of regions in your Cosmos DB account, making it a globally distributed database. This ensures SLAs up to 99.999% for a multiregion write-enabled account.
	The underlying redundancy feature of Cosmos DB ensures that containers are horizontally partitioned, every partition is replicated, all commits are durable, and replicas are distributed across several (up to 20) fault domains. Each region contains all the partitions across regions and can serve both reads and writes.
	You can design multiregion accounts with multiple writes, making it highly available for writes and reads. All regional failovers are quick and do not require any code or configuration change. You can choose between multiregion with single write region or multiregion with multiwrite region.

Azure Key Vault	A single key vault can support multiple applications. Hence, it is of utmost importance that the keys and secrets are kept in a highly resilient and fault-tolerant platform or service. The Azure Key Vault service is not only hosted on a highly resilient platform, but it also replicates the keys, secrets to another location in the same geography at least 150 miles away. In an event wherein one region is unavailable, the requests are routed to the alternate paired region (failover). When the primary region is online again, the requests are sent to the primary region (failback). This is an automatic process and no action is required on the part of the application. For a multigeographical deployment across the world, multiple instances of the service will have to be deployed and necessary service configuration must be performed. Should you need to back up all objects in the key vault, PowerShell scripts can be used to back up and restore every item because there is no built-in backup and restore functionality. Additional considerations should be made to ensure that no data on file is exposed or available publicly and is stored in a secure manner.
Azure Storage	With Azure Storage we have various options to store and recover massive scale and types of data across regions, as we discussed in detail earlier in this chapter.
Azure Virtual Machine	We discussed Azure Virtual Machine earlier. To quickly touch on the high-level constructs, leverage single node resiliency with 99.9% SLA with premium storage. With availability sets you can protect your IaaS workloads against hardware- and network-level failures. Leverage availability zones to sustain datacenter-wide failures. With Microsoft Azure regional pairs of datacenters and ASR, you can replicate and recover your VMs and data across regions.

(continued)

109

Table 3-4. (*continued*)

Service Name	Considerations
Azure Event Hubs	Azure Event Hubs is a massive scale event ingestion service capable of processing multimillions of events per second. It also supports real-time and batch processing. To be able to have durable events and data, and at the same time support outages and failures, Azure Event Hubs supports geo-recovery and availability zones.

When you deploy a new event hub, you can choose to deploy to an availability zone, which makes it fault tolerant against datacenter-level failure. Also, with multinamespace deployment with a *pairing*, an event hub can provide geo-recovery. This includes creating a new or secondary namespace, create a pairing, and defining a trigger to perform a failover. You can refer to the Azure documentation for complete details. |
| Azure Service Bus | Azure Service Bus requires a unique namespace that does not span Azure regions. Hence, we have to create an alternative namespace in the target region, too. However, the name of the topic or entity can be the same in both regions.

The Premium tier and the Basic tier enable various considerations and capabilities. For example, Premium tier supports deployment to availability zones and geo-disaster recovery with primary and secondary namespaces.

As for standard Service Bus, you still need to create two namespaces and can choose between active replication of messages to both the namespaces and to only one. The sender needs to send to both or only one. However, the receiver must read both locations and suppress duplicate messages. If you are using Azure relay, two endpoints must be created in different namespaces. These namespaces should reside in different datacenters. |

Azure Search	Creating redundant instances in multiple regions is currently the only way to build a multiregional DR solution for Azure Search. Redirection and failover logic should be part of the application code. In a typical multiregional scenario, once the failover of the application occurs, the search index will be rebuilt as the application starts serving requests in the target region.
Azure Content Delivery Network (CDN)	Azure CDN is a global service to deliver content through edge locations. Because this is a globally managed service, there are no DR-specific patterns for CDN. You can choose to redeploy a new service if there are instance-specific issues in one region. In the event there is a global service outage, the application should be coded to read from an alternate storage location. For example, the origin of a CDN can be a storage account that has an RA-GRS endpoint, and the application in a CDN outage should be able to read from an RA-GRS location.

(continued)

Table 3-4. (*continued*)

Service Name	Considerations
Azure APIM	For APIM you have these available options to choose from.
	• Service backup and restore. There are backup and restore REST application programming interfaces (APIs) that you can call to back up the configuration and content of an operational APIMs instance. Restoring to another standby instance will help keep two instances in sync. Remember that the restore operation does not change the hostname configuration and you will have to use the same hostname across deployments. Second, it also copies users and subscription information that has to be evaluated carefully.
	• Create a new instance of APIM in the target region. Alternatively, you can create a new instance and configure it during a disaster.
	• You can also deploy APIM with a multiregional deployment wherein requests can be routed to a secondary region in case the primary region is offline.
	The decision completely depends on your RTO and RPO and other functionality requirements. You need to be careful in choosing the approach in case there are multiple applications that depend on the same APIM instance.

Azure Application Gateway	• You achieve DR across multiple datacenters by distributing traffic across a redundant set of application gateways. You should use Azure Traffic Manager to load balance traffic across multiple application gateways deployed in various datacenters.
	• The Application Gateway V2 SKU supports autoscaling and multizone deployment without having to deploy multiple instances in each datacenter.
	• Reduced deployment time helps to deploy such a service across different regions for full-stack infrastructure deployment in the event of an entire regional outage.

Cost Implications

Who can ignore the costs associated with any solution? It is at times the most important constraint against which any solution is designed. A highly available solution with an active recovery site always incurs a higher cost than a passive or standby solution for obvious reasons. Hence, recovery requirements and cost implications should be balanced to derive the best alternatives and options. The choice should always the one that keeps the business running.

Now that we have a fair understanding of the various design considerations, let us look at a few scenarios in which we can put our understanding together to create a DR solution. We explore these scenarios not with a lot of low-level configuration details, but from a high-level architectural solution design perspective. We will explore three types of deployment on Azure-to-Azure DR scenarios.

- A two-tier application that uses Azure VM for its web tier and data tier with cold DR requirements.

- A three-tier application that leverages both IaaS and PaaS services for a warm DR.

- A multitier application that needs to be designed with multiregional deployment for active-active DR.

DR for a Simple Azure VM-Based Application

In this section we look at a simple recovery solution that involves leveraging ASR for Microsoft Azure IaaS VMs and other important design considerations for it.

Scenario

Figure 3-6 depicts a two-tier application (one node each) with Windows Server hosting a web-based application. A SQL Server database houses the data for the application. Both are hosted inside a virtual network in different subnets in the Azure Southeast Asia region. This is an internal application and is one of many that are accessed by on-premises users. There is an existing ExpressRoute connectivity from on-premises to the Azure virtual network which extends the datacenter network. The application houses some of the critical workflow of the business process. Although the application is not required to be highly available, the organization needs to protect the workload from datacenter-wide and regional failures. Let us explore how we can achieve a recovery plan for this application.

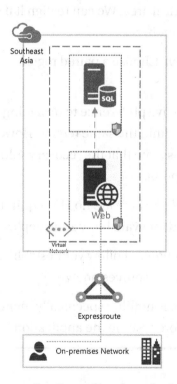

Figure 3-6. *Simple Azure IaaS application deployment architecture*

Recovery Solution

Let us broadly design and plan the recovery solution based on the available information just presented.

In an ideal world, you will probably divide the design and planning phases. The design phase will include the key architectural considerations, key platform design considerations, alternatives, assumptions, the rationale for decision, and decisions. The entire process will vary from organization to organization. In our case, to keep things simple and focused, we discuss these aspects in the following manner. Here are a few key design decisions for the recovery solution.

- *Compliance and data sovereignty:* In the absence of explicit details, we design to keep the data within the same geopolitical area. We can realign it if required before finalization.

- *Recovery region:* Choose a paired region, in this case East Asia.

- *Subscription:* Give preference to designing in a different subscription within the same tenant. However, in this case, we will assume that the recovery solution is in the same subscription.

- *High availability:* There are no HA requirements, and hence no need for availability zone deployments.

- *Naming conventions:* Follow your established naming conventions for resources on Azure.

- *Identity:* There is nothing specifically mentioned; we will therefore assume the application has its own authentication code.

- *Integration:* There are no specific integration details available other than on-premises network integration using ExpressRoute.

- *Network:* All users are internal and access the application from on-premises. Hence, we need to ensure that the recovery site already has stable on-premises connectivity. Establish a network stamp similar to the source or production site before any failover can happen.

- *Firewall and exclusions:* Gather and configure all firewall ports (incoming and outgoing) up front. Azure Network Security groups should have similar inbound and outbound rules.

- *DNS name:* Plan and document the necessary DNS name changes and IP changes to ensure that the application is accessible postfailover.

- *Backup:* This is a simple application with two nodes and Azure Backup is required to ensure recovery from corruption, human error, or any other issues that might cause inconsistencies in the application. Existing backup policies should be reviewed to ensure they are aligned to achieve expected RPO.

- *Replication solution for VM:* If there is a low RTO and RPO requirement, ASR can be used for continuous replication and recover the application in a secondary datacenter in another region. Because both the web and the database are single node standard deployment, we can use ASR to handle replication and failover tasks.

- *Data storage:* There is no additional data storage other than the VM disks. Managed disks will be handled by ASR.

- *Postrecovery customizations:* This could vary depending on the application. For simple applications, it could include only changing the connection string or IP address in the application to point to a new database server, or a required DNS change or URL change to let users access the application from the secondary site.

- *Failback:* Once the VMs are failed over, you need to reprotect them to ensure they replicate back to the primary region. It is important, though, that the VM is in the Failover committed state, the primary region is available, and you are able to create and access new resources in it.

We are not discussing the step-by-step configuration here. Once the entire recovery solution is developed and implemented, we will have two options to recover the application in the event of a disaster.

- *Backup recovery:* Either the tier or systems can be recovered in the same or a different region using cross-region backup restore. You should check the supportability of cross-region restore in your region.

- *Recovery through ASR:* Figure 3-7 depicts the high-level deployment view of the application while configured with ASR for DR. The entire application can be failed over to the East Asia region using Recovery Services. In this case, both the VMs will be protected using ASR for Azure VMs and the target network and subnet and IP configurations will be handled. Once the VMs come online in the target virtual network, postrecovery

customizations (automated or manual) will ensure
that the application tier can access the database. On-
premises users will be able to access the application
(with the same name if configured with CNAME) or
using a new URL.

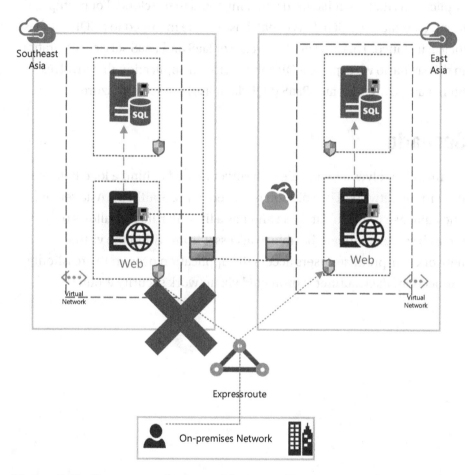

Figure 3-7. *Recovery solution with Azure Site Recovery for a simple*
Azure IaaS application

DR for an Application That Uses IaaS and PaaS Services

We explored a DR solution with ASR in the previous example. However, services could be different for various applications. There are several applications that are refactored when migrated to the cloud. For example, if found compatible, a SQL Server database can be migrated to a SQL database logical instance. This is a very basic case of IaaS and PaaS service integration. In this scenario we explore a DR solution for an application that involves both IaaS (Azure VM) and PaaS (SQL database) services on Azure.

Scenario

Figure 3-8 involves a two-node web server hosted behind a load balancer in a virtual network. The solution is hosted in the Southeast Asia region. The database is a SQL database and has a firewall rule that allows only the web server subnet to be able to access it from within the virtual network. On-premises users access the application over an ExpressRoute connection. Each subnet is protected via network security group.

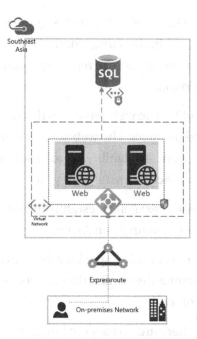

Figure 3-8. *Simple Azure IaaS application with SQL database (PaaS)*

Recovery Solution

We apply the information, knowledge, and structure from the previous scenario and build the recovery solution for this example application.

Here are a few key design decisions for the recovery solution:

- *Compliance and data sovereignty:* In the absence of explicit details, we will design to keep the data within the same geopolitical area. We can realign if required before finalization.

- *Recovery region:* Choose a paired region, in this case East Asia because the primary region is Southeast Asia.

- *Subscription:* Give preference to designing in a different subscription within the same tenant. However, in this case, we will assume that the recovery solution is in the same subscription.

- *High availability:* The web servers in this case are behind a load balancer. The web servers should be placed in the same availability set to ensure hardware-level fault tolerance in the target region.

- *Naming conventions:* Follow established naming conventions for resources on Azure.

- *Identity:* There is nothing specifically mentioned, so we will assume the application has its own authentication code.

- *Integration:* There are no specific integration details available other than on-premises network integration using ExpressRoute.

- *Network:* All users are internal and access the application from on-premises. We therefore need to ensure that the recovery site already has stable in-premises connectivity. Establish a network stamp like the source or production site before any failover can happen.

- *Firewall and exclusions:* Gather and configure all firewall ports (incoming and outgoing) up front. Azure Network Security groups should have similar inbound and outbound rules.

- *DNS name:* Plan and document the necessary DNS name changes and IP changes to ensure that the application is accessible postfailover.

- *Backup:* Azure Backup is required to ensure recovery from corruption, human error, or any other issues that might cause inconsistencies in the application. Existing backup policies should be reviewed to ensure they are aligned to achieve expected RPO. For SQL database, managed backup will be used.

- *Replication solution for VM:* ASR is used for continuous replication and recovery of the application in a secondary datacenter in another region (East Asia in this case).

- *Replication solution for SQL database:* Azure SQL database supports geo-replicated secondary databases. In this case we can create a secondary database in East Asia region.

- *Azure load balancer:* We can either precreate the load balancer or it can be created at the time of recovery. Additional steps will be required to add the recovered servers to the load balancer back-end pool.

- *Data storage:* There is no additional data storage other than the VM disks. Managed disks will be handled by ASR.

- *Postrecovery customizations:* As discussed earlier, this depends on the application. It could include only changing the connection string or IP address in the application to point to a new database server, and required DNS change or URL change to let users access the application from the secondary site.

- *Failback:* Once the VMs are failed over, you need to reprotect them to ensure they replicate back to the primary region. It is important, however, that the VM is in the Failover committed state, the primary region is available, and you are able to create and access new resources in it. Similarly, for SQL database we need to enable geo-replication to the primary region as soon as the region is available for possible failback configuration.

In the event of a disaster we will be able to recover using either of the following options.

- *Backup recovery:* Either of the web systems can be recovered in the same or a different region using cross-region backup restore. You should check the supportability of cross-region restore in your region. Azure SQL database managed backup can be used to recover the database as well.

- *Recovery through ASR:* Figure 3-9 depicts the high-level deployment view of the application while configured with ASR and a SQL database geo-replicated secondary. The entire application can be failed over to the East Asia region using Recovery Services and with automation. In this case, both the VMs will be protected using ASR for Azure VMs and the target network and subnet and IP configurations will be handled. At the time of disaster:

  1. Initiate a failover to the secondary database.

  2. Ensure all network rules are updated already in the target region, including network security groups, SQL database firewall rules to include only the VM subnet, on-premises firewall rules, and so on.

3. A new load balancer is created in the target
    network.

4. Use ASR to failover the VMs and recover the
    application.

5. Change the application connection string
    changes to access the database.

6. Add the VMs to the load balancer
    back-end pool.

7. Add necessary DNS and CNAME changes
    to add the load balancer endpoints to be
    accessible for the users on-premises.

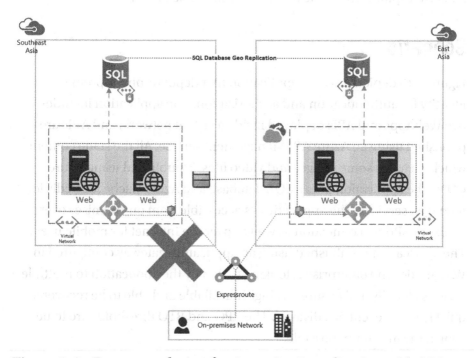

Figure 3-9. *Recovery solution for Azure IaaS application with SQL
database (PaaS)*

The entire process of failover can be automated using the Azure automation runbook and the recovery plan together. You can add multistep automated processes in the recovery plan to invoke the SQL database recovery, validation of NSGs, failover of the VMs in groups, creation of the load balancer, and adding the back ends and updating the connection strings in Azure Key Vault, if in use.

DR for a Multiregional Deployment

In the following scenario we are considering an existing solution that is deployed in a single region involving Azure PaaS and IaaS services. However, an enterprise looking to expand its operation in multiple regions and also explore DR can be achieved in such a scenario.

Scenario

Figure 3-10 depicts a scaled application that depends on on-premises identity for authentication and authorization. The application includes two WebApps and APIs deployed inside a virtual network, and APIs are published using an Azure API Management service. All the static content, which includes some images and video files, is published using Azure CDN. The application uses a SQL database and Azure Cache for Redis for managed services. The application is accessible from on-premises over an ExpressRoute connection as well as over the Internet for mobile users. The application is published using an application gateway configured in a WAF mode. The enterprise is looking to deploy the application to multiple regions globally and ensure it is highly available and able to be recovered quickly in the event of a disaster. The RPO and RTO thresholds are to be kept at the minimum possible.

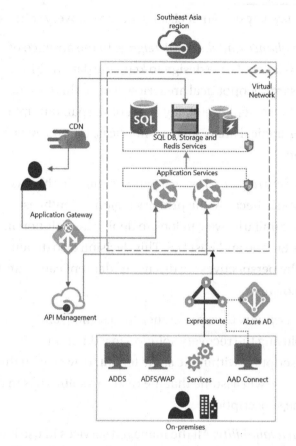

Figure 3-10. *Enterprise application with multiple PaaS services and on-premises integration*

Recovery Solution

In this scenario, we have the entire application developed and deployed leveraging Azure PaaS services. Hence, we need to use the relevant PaaS services' capabilities to design the recovery solution. Let us follow the same structure as earlier examples to create the solution.

Here are a few key design decisions for the recovery solution.

- *Compliance and data sovereignty:* In the absence of explicit details, we design to keep the data within the same geopolitical area. However, in this case to be able to deploy globally, it needs to span multiple geographical areas such as Americas, Europe, Asia, and so on.

- *Recovery region:* Choose a paired region, in this case East Asia because the primary region is Southeast Asia. Similarly, we can look to deploy the solution in East Europe and East U.S. This decision also depends on the perspectives we discuss under replication and deployment.

- *Subscription:* Give preference to designing and deploying the recovery solution in a different subscription within the same tenant. However, in this case, we will assume that the recovery solution is in the same subscription.

- *High availability:* All the managed services in use have inherent HA capabilities. Choose multiple instances for a deployment wherever applicable. For example, select at least two instances for Azure Application Gateway.

- *Naming conventions:* Follow established naming conventions for resources on Azure.

- *Identity:* The application uses on-premises identity, which is synced to Azure Active Directory. We need to ensure Secure Token Services (ADFS) is implemented and configured with domain federation to be able to handle all authentication requests and for true single sign-on experience.

- *Integration:* The on-premises network is integrated using ExpressRoute and hybrid identity is implemented using Azure Active Directory Connect.

- *Network:* There are internal as well as external users for the application. Hence, we need to ensure that the recovery site already has stable in-premises connectivity. Establish a network stamp like the source or production site before any failover can happen. Also, necessary network services such as Application Gateway must be configured up front or before the solution is published to the external users. Network configuration will include IP address segments for all regions, connectivity requirements for all virtual networks, and accessibility requirements for the on-premises users to all the region deployments. For example, assuming the head office or primary location of users is in Southeast Asia, we might not need to have any ExpressRoute connection for other regions of deployment from the on-premises location.

- *Firewall and exclusions:* Gather and configure all firewall ports (incoming and outgoing) up front. Azure Network Security groups should have similar inbound and outbound rules.

- *DNS name:* Plan and document the necessary DNS name changes and IP changes to ensure that the application is accessible postfailover.

- *Backup:* Backup for each application service is required to ensure recovery from corruption, human error, or any other issues that might cause inconsistencies in the application. Existing backup policies should be reviewed to ensure they aligned to achieve the expected RPO. Refer to the Microsoft Azure services documentation site online for the latest features and information. Table 3-5 presents high-level details and perspectives to look at and consider for the application backup solution. The most important aspect is to ensure all critical components are factored in.

Table 3-5. *Application backup considerations*

Service	Backup Option
ExpressRoute	For ExpressRoute, the service provider provides redundancy and SLAs for the connectivity. If your compliance requirement is to ensure an alternative to the ExpressRoute, a site-to-site VPN should be configured. If you are using Windows base servers with Routing and Remote Access (RRAS) roles for gateway services, ensure they are configured with HA. You can also use one of the supported devices as well. A list of such devices can be found at https://docs.microsoft.com/en-us/azure/vpn-gateway/vpn-gateway-about-vpn-devices. You can keep a copy of the VPN configuration in an appropriate blob storage for additional safe keeping.
Virtual Network	Azure Virtual Network is a highly available service. You can create a PowerShell script or an Azure Resource Manager (ARM) template that can deploy the entire network stamp with a single click. No additional backup is required.
Azure Active Directory	Azure Active Directory is a nonregional service and no backup is required.

(continued)

Table 3-5. (*continued*)

Service	Backup Option
Azure Active Directory Connect	You do not need to backup any Azure Active Directory Connect service. We can always redeploy a new server and set up Azure Active Directory Connect if required.
Application Gateway	Application Gateway is a regional resource. Select at least two instances for deployment of the service. Create a script for the configuration to save it to a blob storage.
API Management	You can either deploy multiple instances of this service or restore from a backup. It is worth mentioning that API Management supports multiregional deployments in the premium tier only and should be considered once a cost versus benefit analysis is done. For API Management there is no portal support that will help you to configure and restore from backup. You need to use REST APIs to do that. Here are the high-level steps. • Configure an Azure Active Directory account by registering a new application in Azure Active Directory. • Set permission to grant access to Azure API Management. • Get the token for authentication to Azure Resource Manager. You can refer to Microsoft documentation for complete step-by-step details on how to implement API Management.
App Services	Azure App Services provides managed backup capabilities that you can schedule based on your RTO and RPO requirements. You can also include the SQL database as part of your backup. The size should not exceed 10 GB.

(*continued*)

Table 3-5. (*continued*)

Service	Backup Option
SQL database	Create a backup of the SQL database preferably as part of the application backup or independently.
Storage account	Azure Storage maintains multiple copies of the same data to ensure HA and guard against unexpected failure. However, to safeguard against accidental deletions, you can back up the data at specific intervals using the AzCopy tool.
	You can also develop a sample application that can back up your storage data at specific intervals. The data in the storage account contains flat files and videos that are most likely sourced from another on-premises repository. You can explore options to back up the data at the source instead of backing them up in Azure Storage.
Redis Cache	The premium tier of Azure Cache for Redis supports export and import of the cache data from one instance to another. You can export the data to a storage account, which in turn can be replicated to another region. In our scenario, we can choose to build the cache over a period of time because there are performance-specific requirements. It will be important to use the export-import feature when application performance is part of the service agreement, too.
Content Delivery Network	CDN is a nonregional service and no specific action for backup is required. Based on the configured time-to-live (TTL) values of the objects, they remain in cache, for example, seven days. If the origin (in this case the storage account) or the actual source of the objects is available and backed up, we can leverage them to bring them into CDN.

Postrecovery customizations: This depends on the application deployment choices made, whether multiple regions are in the same geopolitical area or one region is in each geopolitical area, and if the application is designed to be able to initiate API calls across regions. It could also include changing the connection string or IP address in the application to point to a new database server, and required DNS change or URL change to let users access the application from the secondary site. This will be applicable if there is a primary site and secondary site (recovery site) deployment planned for each geography; for example, Asia—East Asia and Southeast Asia; Americas—East U.S. and West U.S.; Europe—East Europe, West Europe.

- *Failback:* For failback planning and design, all activities similar to the original recovery solution have to happen because the entire solution is based on inherent capabilities of the services, and this is a multiregion deployment and recovery planning effort.

- *Replication and deployment:* To minimize RTOs, we can choose among various options, considering cost versus benefit of the solution. Instead of creating a directional and prescriptive solution, we discuss the options and perspectives that will help you to design better. Let us look at a few perspectives now.

Choosing Global Deployment Options

The correct choice of global deployment is a critical decision. In some scenarios, it also should form a part of your software architecture design. For our discussion, let's say Figure 3-10 is a single deployment stamp. We can deploy the same stamp in multiple geographies with at least one stamp each; for example, one deployment each in East U.S., East Europe, and Southeast Asia. This makes the application truly global in terms of deployment stamp. However, the decision will depend on the user base and data sovereignty. If a majority of the users are from the United States and only a limited number of users are from Asia, we might not need several deployments in multiple geopolitical areas. Figure 3-11 depicts a multigeo deployment stamp wherein the data is localized to that region. The solution is highly available but does not conform to any recovery requirement. If the region in the specific geography is unavailable, users in that region will lose access to the data. They can still access the application from the other region.

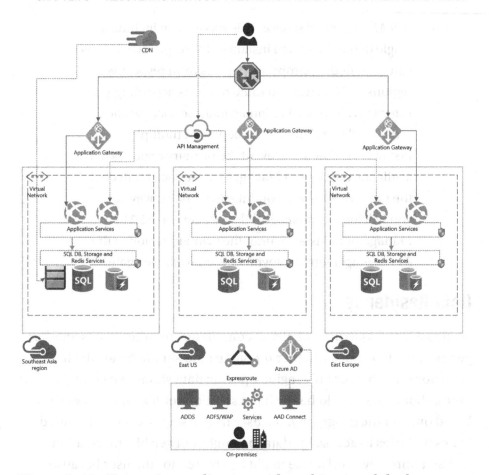

Figure 3-11. *Enterprise application with multiregional deployment with on-premises integration*

There are two additional aspects required for this design to make it global.

- *Traffic Manager service:* To route traffic across various geopolitical areas, we will leverage a Traffic Manager profile. We can either choose geographical mode or performance-based traffic distribution. Each application gateway from each region will form an endpoint or entry point to its respective regions.

- *API Management service:* This service can include a single deployment and instances for respective regions can be added. Appropriate policies from respective regions will be added to route requests accordingly. Alternatively, one API Management service for each region will be required. The benefit of multiple instances is that in the event the primary region is not available and the API Management service is affected, the other regions will continue to work. However, you will lose the manageability aspects of the API Management instance until the primary region of the API Management deployment is unavailable again.

Data Residency

Data residency as a functional and compliance requirement is another perspective. It decides whether the same data should be available in all regions or whether only region-specific data should be enough. Think about what would happy if the solution routes for users were based only on the geography. If a user from Asia travels to the United States and tries to access his data, he might not see his information and an entire new workspace might be created for the user because he does not exist in the region. Second, his data is not available either. Whether you should have a distributed but isolated multiregional deployment or not will be dependent on application functionality requirements and data availability decisions. This has be to be planned from the very beginning of the application design development cycle. This become clearer when we decide whether the application should be able to query across multiple application instances in various deployment stamps or not and what infrastructure support will be required to achieve that. That leads to our third perspective on design and deployment planning. There are lessons from the first perspective and additional enhancement requirements from the second. We can apply both and say we can definitely choose the best of both worlds if we create a recovery site (or recovery region; paired region) for each geographical deployment. That will lead to at least six deployment stamps (one primary and one secondary in each geopolitical area) in total. Whether we need an infrastructure that large or not is another business discussion.

Service Capability and Network Connectivity

The service capability and network connectivity perspective includes several elements.

- What services are available in the deployment regions? Will they be able to match the primary region of deployment to serve users in the event of a disaster?

- What network connectivity will be required to enable such functionalities?

- What infrastructure support has to be enabled for the application in this scenario to invoke APIs in another region?

For our discussion, let us design this for a single geography and with two regions as active-active. Both regions will be serving user requests. All data should be accessible across regions if the user travels. The design will be highly available and recoverable in case of disaster. Table 3-6 describes the core services and their deployment design.

Table 3-6. *Core Services and Their Deployment Details*

Service	Deployment Details
Virtual Network	One virtual network in each region: Southeast Asia and East Asia with similar deployment but with different IP address ranges. Because the deployment will have on-premises integration, IP segments cannot be identical. ExpressRoute connectivity will be established with both regions.
Identity System	Active Directory Federation Service (ADFS) systems will be highly available and backed up on-premises and appropriate recovery steps will be implemented. Azure Active Directory Connect will be redeployed if required.
Traffic Manager	A nonregional service; only one deployment with an appropriate profile based on performance or geography.
Application Gateway	One deployment in each region. Traffic Manager will hold the application service endpoint to route the traffic to a specific region.
API Management	Single deployment in Southeast Asia with added region for East Asia.
Application Service	Application Service will be deployed in both regions and will be active.

(*continued*)

Table 3-6. (*continued*)

Service	Deployment Details
SQL database	To ensure both regions have the same data with minimal latency, we will use SQL Data Sync technology. Data Sync lets us synchronize data bidirectionally across multiple databases and server instance deployments. At the same time, we will also create a read replica of SQL databases to recover from disaster.
Azure Cache for Redis	We will enable geo-replicas of Redis instances across two regions. Both replicas will be active. We can also let the cache be regional and build up if required.
Storage account	We will use one storage account in the primary region only and configure it as GDS because the data load occurs in the primary region and CDN will use this as an origin point. If the primary storage endpoint is not available, the secondary endpoint in the East Asia region will be available to serve as an endpoint for CDN origin.

With these consideration and design factors, the two-region deployment will look like the diagram in Figure 3-12.

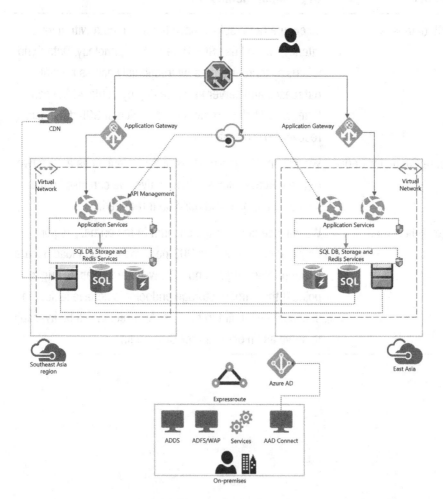

Figure 3-12. *Enterprise application with two-region deployment with on-premises integration*

Great! However, this design does not solve one aspect. Neither of the API web apps from Southeast Asia is able to query Redis Cache and any API app from East Asia. Second, and more important, geo-replication of Redis Cache requires network connectivity between two regions, and this will not work over a simple vNet peering. Redis leverages basic load balancers and by design you cannot access the endpoint of a basic load balancer from another virtual network over a regional vNet peering. It requires site-to-site connectivity. In this case vNet-to-vNet connectivity will be required.

With vNet-to-vNet connectivity, you will be able to access resources across regions. For example, API App A in Southeast Asia will be able to call API App B in East Asia. This opens up several possibilities to make the entire environment more resilient. In the absence of strong monitoring, alerting, logging, and automated or manual actions, there will be user experience issues and unnecessary downtime. Hence, we need to enable the design with such connectivity that allows app services in the Southeast Asia region to be able to access the SQL database and Redis in the other region.

With these above new considerations, our design will look like Figure 3-13.

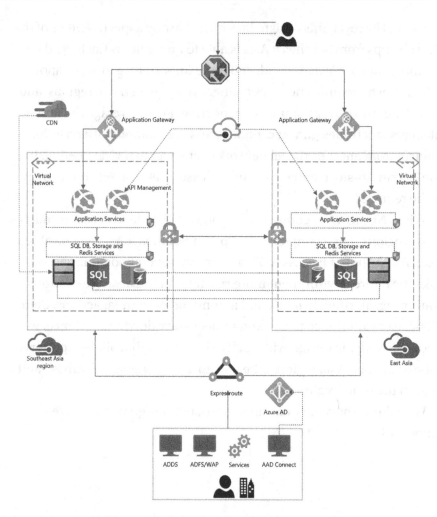

Figure 3-13. *Multiregional deployment with Redis Cache geo-replication*

In the event of a disaster we will be able to recover using either of the following options.

- *Backup recovery:* Either of the web systems can be recovered in the same or different regions using a cross-region backup restore as discussed earlier.

- *HA and recoverability:* With multiregional deployment with cross-site connectivity and each layer and service equipped with geo-replicas, the system should be resilient with single service or multiservice failure. At the same time one region is unavailable, the other region should be able to serve the request with minimal user disruption. In the event of a prolonged outage, another region can be built with the data so it is available in the other region with a similar deployment stamp.

Summary

With Microsoft Azure services and capabilities, you can plan and design your application to be more resilient and fault tolerant. Azure offers various possibilities to plan, design, and deploy based on your business requirements. What we have covered in this chapter is a very high-level perspective on designing recovery solutions for workloads that are on Azure, leveraging various services like storage, networks, Application Gateway, API Management, Redis, ASR, Azure Backup, VMs, and so on. We also looked at systems that integrate with on-premises systems. We looked at multiregional deployments to reach global customers and what aspects we can leverage to create a recovery solution around that aspect. Microsoft Azure Architecture Center is a great resource that you should visit to learn the various best practices and design references for building a truly resilient system. In upcoming chapters, we look at more scenarios and how to create recovery solutions for them.

CHAPTER 4

On-Premises to Azure Disaste Recovery

In this chapter we establish a detailed understanding of scenarios for enterprises looking to building a secondary site (recovery site) on Azure and how ASR can be an important service to achieve this key customer requirement. Eventually it can provide seamless replication and an ideal operational DR solution.

We discuss the current possible scenarios supported by ASR to provide a proper DR solution on Azure for enterprise customers. This solution can avoid all the risks, costs, administration overhead, and other additional challenges encountered when selecting a physical site for DR.

Physical Recovery Site: Risks

Often we miss risk factors and their impact for an organization. In such cases, you might find that an enterprise risk management team will enter the picture. These individuals are responsible for keeping a close watch on the risks involved.

For any organization, whether IT or non-IT, there are common risk areas we should examine before designing or implementing any plans. This is also the key when we undertake business continuity and DR planning for any organization. Table 4-1 provides common risks that we should keep in focus while planning.

© Bapi Chakraborty and Yashajeet Chowdhury 2020
B. Chakraborty and Y. Chowdhury, *Introducing Disaster Recovery with Microsoft Azure*,
https://doi.org/10.1007/978-1-4842-5917-7_4

Table 4-1. *Recovery Site Common Risks*

Risk Classification	Risk Examples
Disaster risk	Storm, tsunami, earthquake
Financial risk	Delayed payment, credit ratings, currency devaluation
Human resource risk	Employee misconduct, labor disputes, workplace accidents and injuries
Market risk	Fierce competitor movement or failure of new product introduction
Environmental risk	Disease, fires, contamination, and leaks
Distribution risk	Transportation carrier failure
Security risk	Terrorism and workplace security
Regulatory risk	Regulatory change or government policy change
Operational risk	Demand uncertainty, poor delivery, poor planning, bad customer service
Safety risk	Workplace accidents and injuries
Supplier risk	Supplier performance failure, rising material costs
IT risk	Failure of software systems or loss of important data

DR plans are a component of business continuity that focus on mitigating the impact of forecasted disasters on specific targeted systems and processes. For unforecasted disasters where no predefined recovery plan is available, the DR plan covers the roles and responsibilities for handling the disaster.

To optimize your business continuity plan to support your IT DR strategy, multiple workshops are necessary. Here we highlight a few of the most important workshops.

- *Kickoff meeting:* Set expectations and provide program information about the goals, planning, and expected outcomes.

- *Service mapping and information gathering:* This workshop collects all information about the business function, service, its components, service owners' details, and so on. Insights gathered in this session are essential in planning for DR.

- *Scenario identification:* Identify possible DR scenarios, impacts, and mitigations that are already in place and probability of the DR scenario that is identified in the meeting. This information will be used to validate the coverage of the technical recovery scenarios and evaluate if the information from the business impact assessment is complete.

- *War room facilities:* Based on the identified recovery scenarios and their constraints, information needs and facility (war room) requirements are identified. It will be crucial to design a strategy that the response can easily run.

- *Responsibility and accountability:* Based on the prior workshops, a Responsibility, Accountable, Consulted and Informed (RACI) assignment matrix will be set up for extending or maintaining the DR plan and running a DR.

Disaster Recovery: Myth vs. Reality and ASR for On-Premises Scenario

There is a myth that you can protect your data by having just having an off-site backup solution implemented in your infrastructure environment for data recovery. A common belief is that if a company is doing backups on- or offsite, they are fully protected, and they can be recovered anytime; that helps to make the environment DR compliant. Unfortunately, people don't think about what will happen if the site goes down. Backups are ineffective at that point in the case of a single point of failure. The cloud allows us to take a copy of your backups and move them offsite, providing a copy of the data in a different location. We can then begin recovery operations while the primary site is down. Really protecting the environment against any type of downtime is only possible by having both a comprehensive backup and DR strategy.

For customers looking for a more orchestrated solution for failover that takes advantage of multiple geographical locations and enables controlled failover between those sites, Microsoft ASR provides a compelling offering. ASR provides a single DR solution that works across platforms (Hyper-V, VMware, physical), across clouds (public, private, and service provider), and across workloads to provide a range of RTO and RPO using multiple channels.

Azure's DR features augment different scenarios with application-specific strategies. Consider some of the many possible causes that lead to a failure during both the design and test phases of a recovery plan. The preferred response is driven by the importance of each application, the recovery objective, and the RTO.

Customers who have multiple sites, or work with a service provider as a secondary site, and have Hyper-V running on both sites can take advantage of ASR to orchestrate replication and recovery between those sites.

Customers who don't have a second site and are running Hyper-V on their primary site can orchestrate the replication and recovery of their on-premises workloads into the Microsoft Azure datacenters using ASR, enabling this as a target for failover in the event of a disaster.

Planning and Design Before Execution

Azure Deployment Planner

The ASR Deployment Planner tool helps enterprise customers understand their on-premises networking requirements, Microsoft Azure computing and storage requirements for successful ASR replication, and test failover or failover of their applications. The ASR Deployment Planner is a command-line tool that is available for VMware- and Hyper-V-to-Azure scenarios.

The tool provides the following capabilities.

- Compatibility assessment

  - A VM eligibility assessment, based on number of disks, disk size, Input/Output Operations Per Second (IOPS), churn, and boot type (EFI/BIOS).

  - The estimated network bandwidth required for delta replication.

- Network bandwidths need vs. RPO assessment

  - The estimated network bandwidth required for delta replication.

  - The throughput that Site Recovery can get from on-premises to Azure.

- The number of VMs to batch, based on the estimated bandwidth to complete initial replication in each amount of time.

- Depending on the replication data and RPO required, we should select a consistent, dedicated, high-bandwidth provider ExpressRoute network; alternatively, we can select the site-to-site VPN.

- Azure infrastructure requirements

  - The storage type (standard or premium storage account) requirement for each VM.

  - The total number of standard and premium storage accounts to be set up for replication.

  - Storage account naming suggestions, based on Azure Storage guidance.

  - The storage account placement for all VMs.

  - The number of Azure cores to be set up before test failover or failover on the subscription.

  - The Azure VM-recommended size for each on-premises VM.

- On-premises infrastructure requirements

  - The required number of configuration servers and process servers to be deployed on-premises.

The tool has three modes:

- *Profiling:* It connects to the vCenter server/vSphere ESXi or Hyper-V host to collect performance data about the VM.

- *Report generation:* The tool generates a macro-enabled Microsoft Excel file (.xlsm file) as the report output, which summarizes all the deployment recommendations.

- *Get throughput:* This is used to estimate the throughput that ASR can achieve from on-premises to Azure during replication.

First, run the tool in profiling mode to gather VM data churn and IOPS. Next, run the tool to generate the report to find the network bandwidth and storage requirements. The tool runs without installing the ASR Deployment Planner components in the on-premises server.

Create a Recovery Services Vault

A Recovery Services Vault is required for ASR. This vault can also be used for Azure Backup services. The Azure Recovery Services Vault is an Azure Resource Manager (ARM) resource that manages customers' backup and DR needs natively in the cloud. Azure Recovery Services Vault has some important features and functionality that fulfill two goals of any enterprise's data protection, data backup and DR. Using Azure Recovery Services Vault features, we can quickly position it as a data protection solution for any enterprise business group. To create a recovery vault, select the Backup and Site Recovery service in Azure. The following are a few of the important functionalities.

- Recovery Services Vault stores data in Azure datacenters, so backup, recovery, and data replication between VMs and the Recovery Services Vault is quick and efficient, depending on the network bandwidth and network medium.

- It provide ease of backup and recovery methods with better user interfaces.

- It meets all major standard certifications including the General Data Protection Regulation (GDPR) requirements, so when data resides in the Recovery Services Vault, that data is encrypted and protected against data attacks.

- It provides built-in functionality for both file and folder backup and the backup of entire VMs.

- It serves nearly all requirements in its default state with less customization.

Manage Network Bandwidth Usage for On-Premises to Azure Protection

Microsoft Azure Recovery Services Agent is installed as a part of enabling ASR for the on-premises environment protection from DR on the Hyper-V host for on-premises VMM or Hyper-V site to Azure. By default it is configured to use the default Internet bandwidth usage settings, but we can configure individual Hyper-V hosts to use different network bandwidth settings.

- Increase bandwidth usage for replicating into Azure by using Registry Editor to locate the following registry key, and then add the following registry entry, or change it if the value already exists:

  HKEY_LOCAL_MACHINE\SOFTWARE\Microsoft\
  Windows Azure Backup\Replication

  Value Name: UploadThreadsPerVM
  Value Type: REG_DWORD
  Value Data: 8

  The agent is configured with a default value of 4, and the maximum supported value is 32.

- Increase bandwidth usage during Azure to on-premises
  failover using the previously mentioned registry
  location and change the value of this key:

```
Value Name: DownloadThreadsPerVM
Value Type: REG_DWORD
Value Data: 8
```

Throttling bandwidth usage for replication by using
PowerShell. The Set-OBMachineSetting cmdlet
configures settings for the server that include proxy
settings for accessing the Internet and network
bandwidth throttling settings. The following sample
cmdlet throttles bandwidth on Mondays and
Tuesdays from 9:00 a.m. to 6:00 p.m.

```
$mon = [System.DayOfWeek]::Monday

$tue = [System.DayOfWeek]::Tuesday

Set-OBMachineSetting -WorkDay $mon, $tue
-StartWorkHour "9:00:00" -EndWorkHour
"18:00:00" -WorkHourBandwidth (512*1024)
-NonWorkHourBandwidth (2048*1024)
```

- We can even choose for a specific server not to use
  network bandwidth throttling by using the command
  Set-OBMachineSetting -NoThrottle.

Setting Up Networking Resources for Test Failover

Networking resources are key components to consider while planning for
ASR in any type of scenario. Setting up the network that is required for test
failover is important and should be available for every replicated item. For
example, in configuring the network mapping, you can select the targeted

network as showcased in Figures 4-1 and 4-2. These settings are optional, but if you skip them, normal behavior will be applied, where you can select the Azure virtual network at the time of triggering test failover.

Figure 4-1. *Azure Site Recovery network mapping*

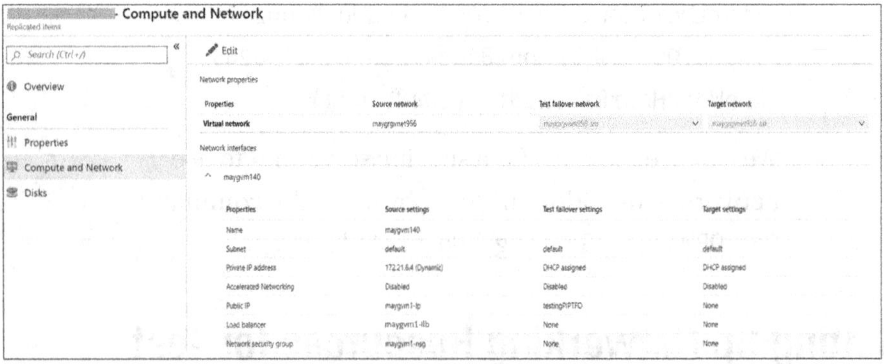

Figure 4-2. *Azure Site Recovery Compute and Network settings*

We can go to the Network settings and choose a test failover target network, in addition to updating all the networking settings for each NIC, as shown in Figure 4-3. The settings only allow you to choose a networking resource that is already created in the target location. ASR does not replicate the changes on networking resources at the source.

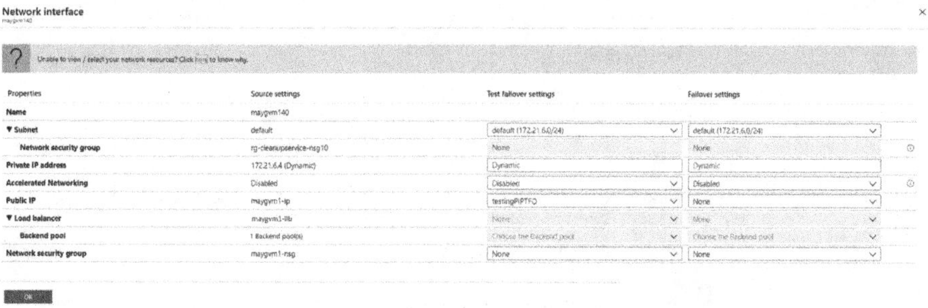

Figure 4-3. *Specific VM network interface configuration for test failover or failover*

In a scenario where we have VMware and physical machines or Hyper-V (without SCVMM) VMs, we can specify the target virtual network for individual VMs, too (see Figure 4-4). In the case of SCVMM managed Hyper-V VMs, though, we use network mapping to map VM networks on a source VMM server and target Azure networks.

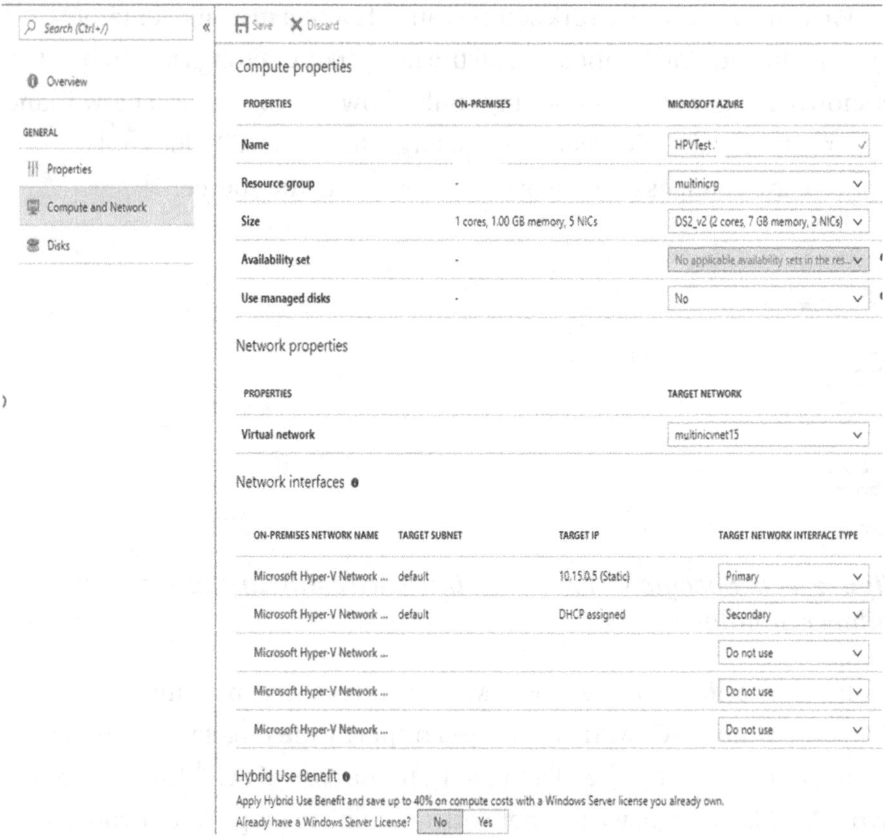

Figure 4-4. *Selecting target network interface for replicated VMs hosted on Hyper-V*

Once you modify the target network, it affects all network interfaces for that specific VM. In the case of the SCVMM cloud, however, modifying network mapping affects all VMs and their network interfaces.

Select the Target Interface Type

When we enable replication, by default ASR selects all detected network interfaces on the on-premises server and marks one as primary and the others as secondary. When we add more network interfaces, we must ensure that the correct Azure VM target size is selected to accommodate all required network interfaces.

Modify Network Interface Settings

You can modify the subnet and IP address for a replicated item's network interfaces as shown in Figure 4-5. If an IP address is not specified, Site Recovery will assign the next available IP address from the subnet to the network interface at failover.

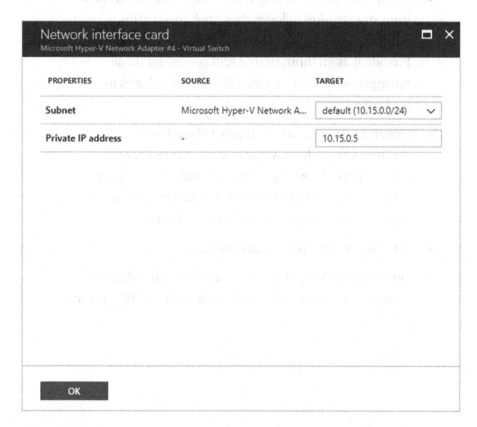

Figure 4-5. *Modifying network interface settings for Hyper-V base replicated VMs*

Common Prerequisites and Configurations

The following is the recommended list of prerequisites before implementing ASR-based DR solutions.

- Create a Recovery Services Vault.

- Set up an Azure network. When Azure VMs are created from storage after failover, they are joined to this network. Create the networking resources in advance. Provide it as an input so that ASR can honor these settings and ensure that the failover VM adheres to these settings.

- Create a storage account. Images of replicated machines are held in Azure storage. Azure VMs are created from the storage when you fail over from on-premises to Azure. The storage account must be in the same region as the Recovery Services Vault.

- Write to the selected storage account.

- Open the Service URLs from the firewall end. Table 4-2 outlines the connectivity requirements for the ASR servers.

Table 4-2. *ASR Connectivity Requirements*

URLs	VMM to VMM	VMM to Azure	Hyper-V Site to Azure	VMware to Azure
*.accesscontrol.windows.net	Access required	Access required	Access required	Access required
*.backup.windowsazure.com		Access required	Access required	Access required
*.hypervrecoverymanager.windowsazure.com	Access required	Access required	Access required	Access required
*.store.core.windows.net	Access required	Access required	Access required	Access required
*.blob.core.windows.net		Access required	Access required	Access required
https://www.msftncsi.com/ncsi.txt	Access required	Access required	Access required	Access required
https://dev.mysql.com/get/archives/mysql-5.5/mysql-5.5.37-win32.msi				Access required

Azure Site Recovery Capacity Deployment Planning

There are several components to consider for capacity planning when using ASR to determine if additional resources will be required. The source environment will encompass the capacity planning for the source machines like maximum daily rate of change and the maximum throughput. There needs to be enough bandwidth for the initial replication and the delta replication.

We can use the ASR Deployment Planner tool, which is a command-line tool. It can be run without installing any Site Recovery components on-premises. It works well for the on-premises-to-Azure scenarios such as for both Hyper-V-to-Azure and VMware-to-Azure DR scenarios. We can even remotely profile the VMware VMs using this tool with no production impact and to understand the bandwidth and storage requirements regarding the replication and failover. Let's understand how and what details we can achieve using this tool.

Network Bandwidth Need vs. RPO Assessment

As mentioned earlier, one of the parameters you can determine is the network bandwidth requirement details to gauge the replication and test failover scenario.

- Throughput that Site Recovery can get from on-premises to Azure.

- Number of VMs to batch, based on the estimated bandwidth to complete the initial replication time window.

- Estimates of network bandwidth required for delta replication.

- RPO that can be achieved for a given bandwidth.

- Impact on the desired RPO if lower bandwidth is provisioned.

Initial Replication Batching Guidance

- Number of VM batches to be used for protection.

- List of VMs in each batch.

- Order in which each batch is to be protected.

- Estimated time to complete initial replication of each batch.

Azure Infrastructure Requirements

- Storage type; whether standard or premium storage is required for each VM.

- Total number of standard and premium storage accounts to be planned and set up for replication, which includes cache storage accounts.

- Storage account naming suggestions, based on Storage guidance.

- Plan for the number of Azure cores to be set up before test failover or failover for a specific subscriptionso you can plan accordingly the Azure subscription quota support.

- Plan on the Azure VM-recommended size for each on-premises VM, which will match the exact performance needed to run the respective VM on Azure.

On-Premises Infrastructure Requirements

- Determine the required number of configuration servers and process servers to be deployed on-premises, depending on the number of servers planned for the DR.

Estimated Disaster Recovery Cost to Azure

- Measure the estimated total DR cost to Azure: compute, storage, network, and Site Recovery license cost. We can substantially control cost only if we opt for Azure hybrid benefits.

- Detail the cost analysis per VM.

Requirements for Replicating Hyper-V Virtual Machines

Table 4-3 outlines the core requirements for replicating Hyper-V VMs using ASR.

Table 4-3. *Hyper-V Core Requirements*

Component	Replicate to Azure (with VMM)	Replicate to Azure (without VMM)	Replicate to Secondary Site (with VMM)
Internet connectivity	From the VMM server and Hyper-V hosts.	From the Hyper-V hosts.	On the VMM server only.
Azure account	You'll need an Azure account and subscription.	Not applicable.	You'll need an Azure account and subscription.
Azure Storage	You'll need an Azure Storage account to store replicated data. Replicated data is stored in Azure Storage and Azure VMs are spun up when failover occurs.	Not applicable.	You'll need an Azure Storage account to store replicated data. Replicated data is stored in Azure Storage and Azure VMs are spun up when failover occurs.

(continued)

Table 4-3. *(continued)*

Component	Replicate to Azure (with VMM)	Replicate to Azure (without VMM)	Replicate to Secondary Site (with VMM)
Network mapping	Set up network mapping so that all machines that fail over on the same Azure network can connect to each other, irrespective of which recovery plan they are in. If there's a network gateway on the target Azure network, VMs can also connect to on-premises VMs. If you don't set up network mapping, only machines that fail over in the same recovery plan can connect.	Not applicable.	Set up network mapping so that VMs are connected to appropriate networks after failover, and replica VMs are optimally placed on target Hyper-V host servers. If you don't configure network mapping, replicated machines won't be connected to any VM network after failover.

(continued)

Table 4-3. *(continued)*

Component	Replicate to Azure (with VMM)	Replicate to Azure (without VMM)	Replicate to Secondary Site (with VMM)
Storage mapping	Not applicable.	Not applicable.	You can optionally set up storage mapping to make sure that VMs are optimally connected to storage after failover (by default, the replica VM will be stored in the location indicated on the target Hyper-V server).
VMM	One or more VMM servers running on System Center 2012 R2. The VMM server should have at least one cloud containing one or more VMM host groups.	Not applicable.	At least one VMM server running on System Center 2012 R2. We recommend a VMM server in each site. The VMM server should have at least one cloud containing one or more VMM host groups. Clouds should have the Hyper-V capability profile set.

(continued)

Table 4-3. *(continued)*

Component	Replicate to Azure (with VMM)	Replicate to Azure (without VMM)	Replicate to Secondary Site (with VMM)
Hyper-V	One or more Hyper-V host servers in the on-premises datacenter running at least Windows Server 2012 R2. The Hyper-V server must be in a host group in a VMM cloud.	One or more Hyper-V servers in the source and target sites running at least Windows Server 2012 R2.	One or more Hyper-V servers in the source and target sites running at least Windows Server 2012 with the latest updates. The Hyper-V server must be in a host group in a VMM cloud.
VMs	You'll need at least one VM on the source Hyper-V server. VMs replicating to Azure must conform with Azure VM prerequisites.	At least one VM on the source Hyper-V server. VMs replicating to Azure must conform with Azure VM prerequisites.	At least one VM in the source VMM cloud.
	Install or upgrade Integration Services in the VM using the steps given here.	Install or upgrade Integration Services in the VM using the steps given here.	Install or upgrade Integration Services in the VM using the steps given here.

(continued)

Table 4-3. *(continued)*

Component	Replicate to Azure (with VMM)	Replicate to Azure (without VMM)	Replicate to Secondary Site (with VMM)
Providers/ Agents	During deployment, you'll install the ASR Provider on VMM servers and the Azure Recovery Services Agent on Hyper-V host servers. The Provider communicates with ASR. The Agent handles data replication between source and target Hyper-V servers. Nothing is installed on VMs.	During deployment, you'll install both the ASR Provider and the Azure Recovery Services Agent on a Hyper-V host server or cluster. Nothing is installed on VMs.	During deployment, you'll install the ASR Provider on VMM servers to communicate with Azure Site Recovery. Replication occurs between Hyper-V source and target servers over the LAN/VPN.
Provider/ Agent connectivity	If the Provider will connect to the Site Recovery service via a proxy, you'll need to make sure the proxy can access the Site Recovery URLs.	If the Provider will connect to Site Recovery via a proxy, you'll need to make sure the proxy can access the Site Recovery URLs.	If the Provider will connect to Site Recovery via a proxy, you'll need to make sure the proxy can access the Site Recovery URLs as mentioned in the earlier section "Common Prerequisites and Configurations."

Requirements for Replicating VMware VMs and Physical Servers

Table 4-4 outlines the core requirements for replicating VMware VMs and physical servers using ASR.

Table 4-4. *VMware Core Requirements*

Component	Replicate to Azure (Enhanced)
Azure account	You'll need an Azure account and subscription.
Azure Storage	You'll need an Azure Storage account to store replicated data. Replicated data is stored in Azure Storage and Azure VMs are spun up when failover occurs.
Azure virtual network	You'll need an Azure virtual network that Azure VMs will connect to when failover occurs. To fail back after failover, you'll need a VPN connection (or Azure ExpressRoute) set up from the Azure network to the on-premises site.
Connectivity	If the management server will connect to Site Recovery via a proxy, you'll need to make sure the proxy server can connect to specific URLs.
On-premises primary site	You install a management server that runs all the Site Recovery components (configuration, process, master target).
On-premises secondary site	Not applicable.
VMware vCenter/ESXi	If you're replicating VMware VMs (or want to fail back physical servers) in your primary site, you'll need a vSphere ESX/ESXi in your primary site. We also recommend a vCenter server to manage your ESXi hosts.

(continued)

Table 4-4. *(continued)*

Component	Replicate to Azure (Enhanced)
Failback	You need a VMware environment to fail back from Azure, even if you're replicating physical servers. The configuration server acts as a master target server, but if you're failing back large traffic volumes you might want to set up an additional on-premises master target server.
Protected machines	At least one VMware VM or physical Windows or Linux server. During deployment, the Mobility service is installed on each machine you want to replicate.

Scenario 1: On-Premises (Hyper-V) to Azure

In this section we are going to dive deep to understand the major considerations in terms of planning, requirements, and general procedures to install and configure the ASR service to protect on-premises VMs using Azure as a target location with your assigned Microsoft Azure subscription. This deployment scenario is particularly useful if you have Hyper-V servers but VMM is not deployed.

Architecture and Planning

This scenario consists of VMs running on on-premises Hyper-V servers or a cluster not managed by SCVMM. The Hyper-V servers will send the configuration and orchestration information in addition to the replicated data from the VMs. Figure 4-6 illustrates the architecture of on-premises Hyper-V to Azure replication. In this architecture the Microsoft Azure Site Recovery (MASR) Agent will be installed on the Hyper-V server that is responsible for replicating data to Azure.

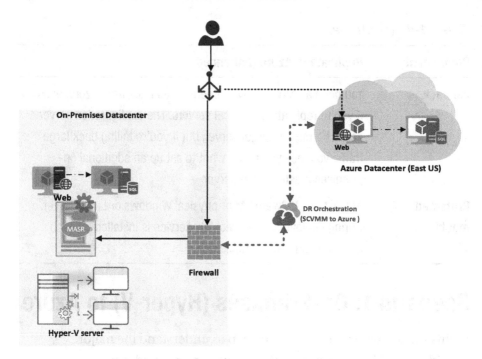

Figure 4-6. *Basic on-premises Hyper-V to Azure replication and DR architecture*

Prerequisites

There are prerequisites (subscription, virtual network, etc.) for using ASR. There are also prerequisites for the on-premises Hyper-V and protected servers. The following are some notable considerations when implementing this step.

- The infrastructure requires Hyper-V hosts running Windows Server 2012 R2 or Windows Server 2016 that have the latest updates installed.

- The Hyper-V hosts require Windows Identity Foundation, .NET Framework 4 & 4.5, and Windows PowerShell.

- Premium storage is not supported yet.

- Protecting Linux VMs with a static IP address is not supported.

- A mixture of Hyper-V hosts running Windows Server 2012 R2 and Windows Server 2016 is not currently supported.

Set Up the Source and Target Environment

First we have to consider planning, selecting, and configuring the source and target environment by setting protection goals and installing and configuring the ASR Provider and the Azure Recovery Services Agent on the Hyper-V server(s). There are some critical considerations in implementing this step.

- Plan, create, and verify that a storage account and virtual network are in place.

- The Hyper-V server agents need access to the Azure URLs specified in the prerequisites. A proxy connection can be configured to allow this connectivity.

- There are command-line installation options for both agents with examples in the documentation.

- If you receive the error "Hyper-V Replica Cluster Broker is not installed," install update rollup 2962409, which can be found at https://support.microsoft.com/en-us/kb/2961977.

- If you're installing on a Hyper-V cluster, run the setup on each cluster node. Installing and registering each Hyper-V cluster node ensures that VMs remain protected even if they migrate across nodes.

The following initial steps are needed to configure while building the on-premises Hyper-V to Azure DR solution.

1. Select a replication goal as shown in Figure 4-7.

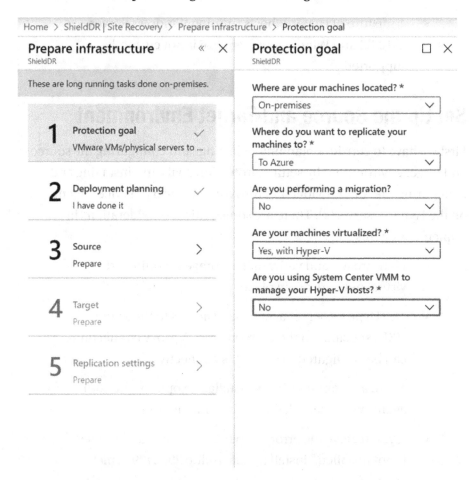

Figure 4-7. *Selecting the protection goal for Hyper-V to Azure replication*

2. Configure replication and prepare the infrastructure. We must prepare the source and target environment.

3. Set up the source replication environment,
    including on-premises Site Recovery components
    and the target replication environment.

•   On the Hyper-V Host server, download and run the
    Microsoft Azure Site Recovery Provider. Once you are
    done with the installation of the ASR Provider, you need
    to proceed with vault registration. After performing the
    registration, you can now see the Hyper-V server in the
    portal. Figures 4-8 and 4-9 display the procedure for
    setting up the Hyper-V site for replication using ASR
    and the verification of the same once the registration to
    the Recovery Services Vault is successfully executed.

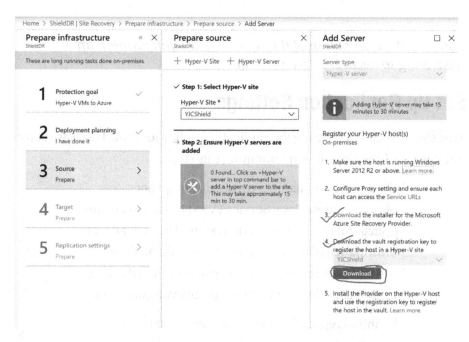

Figure 4-8. *Reference for setting up Hyper-V site and downloading the registration key*

Shield
Hyper-V server

◯ Refresh Server   Renew Certificates   Error Details   🗑 Delete

Name	Shield
Server ID	3912bee5-2dc2-4d2e-9ec7-ddaf307b0dbc
Hyper-V Site	ShieldSite
Connection status	✅ Connected
Last heartbeat	3/18/2020, 9:19:47 PM
Agent version	5.1.5400.0 (latest)
Protected items	1

Figure 4-9. *Verification of the Hyper-V site configuration after registering to Recovery Services Vault*

Set Up Replication Settings

This step consists of creating the replication policy for ASR. There are some notable considerations in implementing this step.

- When using application-consistent snapshots, Volume Shadow Copy Service (VSS) is used to ensure applications are in a consistent state. This will affect the performance of the applications running on the source VMs and ensure that the value you set is less than the number of additional recovery points you configure.

- The initial replication does not have to start immediately and can be scheduled for a later time (e.g., after business hours).

- Replication policies are associated with the Hyper-V site.
  The same replication policy can be applied to multiple
  Hyper-V sites. Replication policies are used to define
  certain parameters to obtain your desired RTO and
  RPO. Replication policies are similar across supported
  types with some differences. With Hyper-V, you must
  specify a copy frequency of either 30 seconds or 5 minutes
  for recovery points. Hyper-V allows for up to 24 hours,
  and all others can allow up to 72 hours of retention. We
  also need to select an app-consistent snapshot frequency.
  App-consistent snapshots capture disk data, all data in
  memory, and all transactions in process.

Here's how to implement this step.

1. Create a recovery plan. To set up replication we first
   need to create a recovery plan and select the VMs
   that we want to replicate as a part of the recovery
   plan on to Azure, as shown in Figure 4-10.

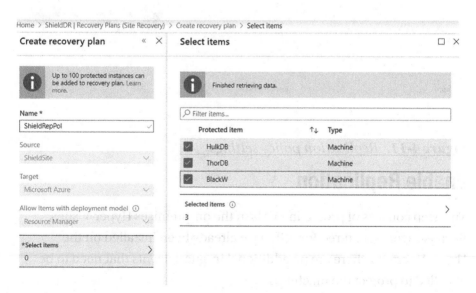

Figure 4-10. *Recovery plan and selecting the set of VMs for replication*

2.   Create a replication policy. After the recovery plan is
     created, we must configure the replication policy where
     we should modify the replication frequency, recovery
     point retention, application consistency as per the
     application criticality, and application team requirements
     we have agreed on. For reference, refer to Figure 4-11.

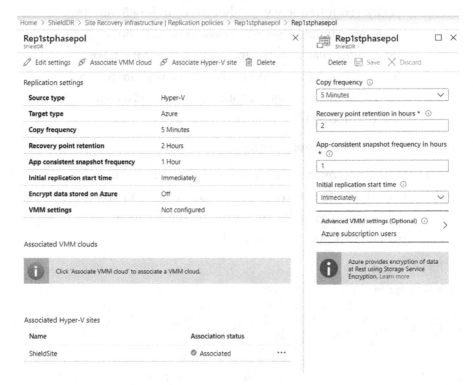

Figure 4-11.   *Replication policy settings*

Enable Replication

This step consists of protecting VMs in the on-premises Hyper-V sites.
Because agents required for ASR have already been installed on the
Hyper-V servers, there are no additional in-guest agents that need to be
installed to protect the machines.

ASR will automatically map the protected on-premises VM to an Azure size (e.g., A6, DS3, etc.). It is recommended that you review the size after a machine is protected.

1. Set up and enable replication for a VM and select the operating system type as shown in Figure 4-12 and Figure 4-13.

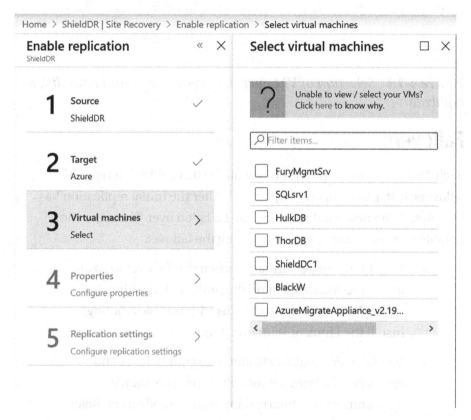

Figure 4-12. *Selection of VMs and enabling the VMs for protection*

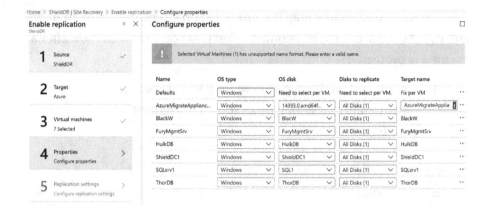

Figure 4-13. Selection of VM operating system type and data disk to replicate

Failovers

Each ASR scenario supports some or all the three different types of failovers: test, planned, and unplanned. After the initial replication has completed, the protected machine can be failed over. There are some notable considerations when performing the failover.

- To get the best performance when you failover to Azure, install the Azure Agent on the protected machine. It makes booting faster and helps with troubleshooting. Install the Linux or Windows Agent.

- Test failover capability to simulate your failover and recovery processes without affecting your source environment and interrupting regular replication. Refer to Figure 4-14.

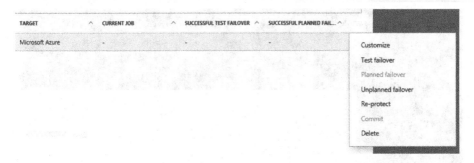

Figure 4-14. *Select test failover to simulate the disaster recovery process*

- Ensure the machines are configured for remote access (e.g., Secure Shell (SSH), Remote Desktop Protocol (RDP)) so they can be managed after a failover. Figure 4-15 shows an unplanned failover and Figure 4-16 shows the status right after execution of the unplanned failover.

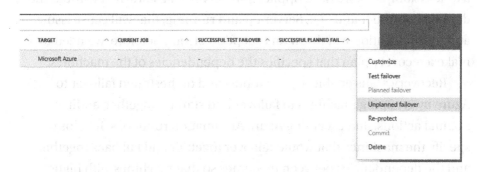

Figure 4-15. *Unplanned failover to Azure*

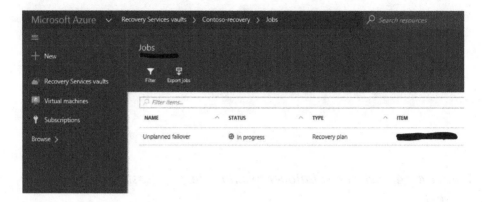

Figure 4-16. *Failover execution status*

Recovery Plans

The fundamental point of having a recovery plan is to restrict the random start of the VMs when failover happens and to control the factors that affect many machines or the dependency life cycle. Let us understand this with a quick example. If we have Application Server that starts first without the domain controller and SQL Server up and running, that will cause issues and the application will throw an exception error. Therefore, we need to make a recovery plan that specifies the dependencies of the machines.

Recovery plans enable a more robust and orchestrated failover to Azure by grouping machines to failover and start up together, adding manual actions, and executing Azure Automation runbooks. It helps to specify the machines that would fail over together and fail back together and the dependencies between machines so that machines with higher priorities, such as domain controllers, start first. The rest of the servers or group of servers can then start as per the defined sequence. Refer to Figure 4-17.

All VMs in the same recovery plan will be placed into the same resource group. In the future, ASR will have additional integration with resource groups.

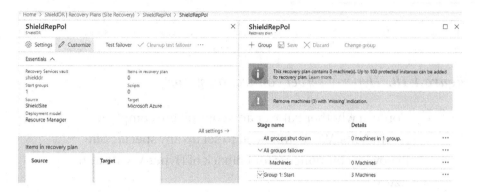

Figure 4-17. *Recovery plan and group*

Failback Solution

Now think about the scenario when our primary datacenter is back
online, in this case the on-premises site. In such a case we consider the
failback scenario. If the failover direction is from Azure to on-premises,
it is considered a failback. We can fail back Hyper-V VMs from Azure by
running a planned failover from Azure to the on-premises site. Because the
VMs are always available on Azure, failback from Azure is always a planned
activity. We can plan for and open a change request window and accept a
short downtime so that workloads can start running on-premises again.

- Failback of Hyper-V VMs replicated using managed
  disks isn't supported. Make sure Azure VMs are using a
  Storage account.

- Make sure the on-premises Hyper-V host or cluster
  is running and constantly connected to Azure. We
  can verify by checking the site status as shown in
  Figure 4-18. If the connection status is Not connected
  as in Figure 4-18, we must troubleshoot the issue,
  re-establish the connectivity, and then initiate the
  failback.

181

Server name	↑↓	Connection status	↑↓	Last heartbeat	↑↓	Agent version	↑↓	Server type	↑↓
Shield		⊗ Not connected		3/19/2020, 12:54:28 AM		5.1.5400.0 (latest)		Hyper-V server	

Figure 4-18. *Hyper-V server connection status*

- Confirm whether failover and commit are complete for the VMs. We do not need to set up any specific Site Recovery components for failback of Hyper-V VMs from Azure.

- Data synchronization and starting the on-premises VM depends on several factors. We can configure the Microsoft Recovery Services Agents to use more threads to parallelize the download by using network bandwidth throttling.

- Planned failback turns off the VMs in Azure and downloads the latest changes. No data loss is expected.

When we want to perform the failover from Azure to your datacenter as shown in Figure 4-19 and Figure 4-20, if our data is lost, we still can choose to create a new VM in our on-premises datacenter, on a specific host. When the process is completed, we must to validate the VM and commit the failover.

Figure 4-19. *Failover back to primary site (on-premises datacenter)*

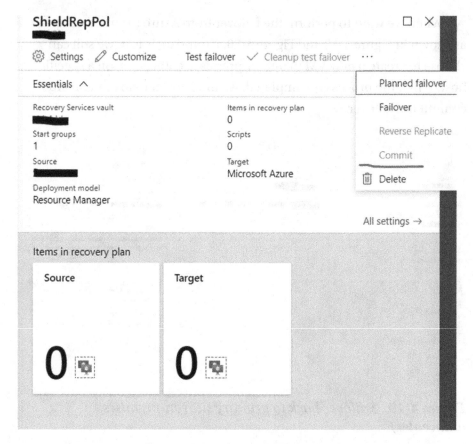

Figure 4-20. Commit option to make the failback successful

This is not yet the final stage that confirms the replication back to on-premises operations. To achieve that we must select the Reverse Replicate option shown in Figure 4-21. Only this option will turn the replication back on-premises.

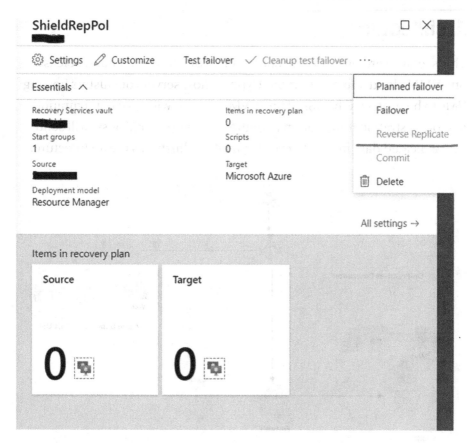

Figure 4-21. *Reverse replication*

Scenario 2: On-Premises Hyper-V Managed by SCVMM to Azure

Use the following general procedures to install and configure the ASR service to protect on-premises VMs using Azure as a target location using your assigned Microsoft Azure subscription. This scenario is commonly referred to as the ASR E-to-A or enterprise-to-Azure scenario. The purpose is to become familiar with the process required to set up and configure the Microsoft Azure, SCVMM, and Hyper-V environment to use the capabilities of the ASR service.

Architecture

This scenario architecture will consist of an SCVMM server and at least one VMM cloud and one or more Hyper-V host servers or clusters hosting VMs to be protected by ASR. The SCVMM server will send configuration and orchestration information to Azure and the Hyper-V hosts will send the replicated data from the VMs. Figure 4-22 illustrates the architecture.

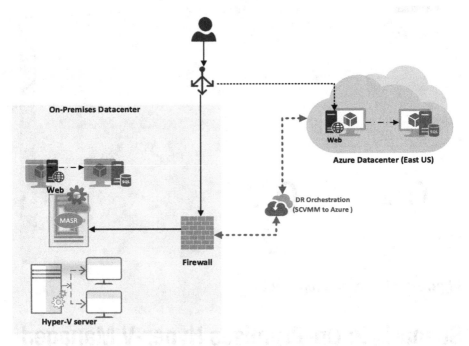

Figure 4-22. *On-premises Hyper-V managed by SCVMM to Azure DR architecture*

Prerequisites

The following are the prerequisites for the on-premises VMM, Hyper-V, and protected servers to replicate on Azure and some major considerations while planning and implementing this scenario.

- The infrastructure requires System Center 2012 R2 or SCVMM 2016 and Hyper-V hosts running Windows Server 2012 R2 with the latest updates installed.

- The VM networks on the source VMM servers should be mapped to the target Azure networks to enable a better failover connectivity experience. More information on network mapping can be found at `https://azure.microsoft.com/en-us/documentation/articles/site-recovery-network-mapping/`.

- The Hyper-V hosts require Windows Identity Foundation, .NET Framework 4 & 4.5, and Windows PowerShell.

- Premium storage is not supported yet.

- Protecting Linux VMs with a static IP address is not supported.

- A mixture of Hyper-V hosts running Windows Server 2012 R2 and Windows Server 2016 is not currently supported.

Set Up the Source and Target Environment

This step consists of setting the protection goals and installing and configuring the Azure Site Recovery Provider on the VMM server and the Azure Recovery Services Agent on the Hyper-V hosts (see Figure 4-23). If we look at the SCVMM managed on-premises virtualized environment DR plan and implementation to Azure using the ASR service, then the whole architecture can be broadly containerized as per the following architecture.

Here are some important considerations before implementation.

- The VMM and Hyper-V server agents need access to the Azure URLs specified in the prerequisites and a proxy connection can be configured to allow this connectivity.

- If you enable data encryption, accept or modify the location of a Secure Sockets Layer (SSL) certificate that is automatically generated for data encryption. This certificate is used for encryption for a cloud protected by Azure in the ASR portal. Keep this certificate safe. When you run a fail over to Azure, you'll need it for decryption if data encryption is enabled.

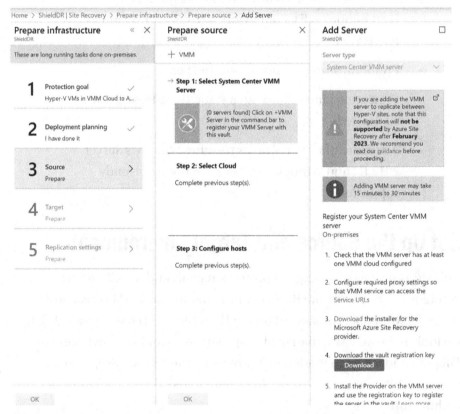

Figure 4-23. *Prepare the source and target for the SCVMM managed Hyper-V replication*

Set Up Replication Settings

One of the importatnt points to consider while implementing these steps is that replication policies are associated with VMM clouds, and the same policy can be replicated to multiple VMM clouds.

Enable Replication

As we discussed earlier, this section is all about protecting VMs in the on-premises VMM clouds. Because agents required for ASR have already been installed on the VMM and Hyper-V servers, there are no additional in-guest agents that need to be installed to protect the machines. ASR will automatically map the protected on-premises VM to an Azure size (e.g., A6, DS3, etc.). You should review the size after a machine is protected. Once you have protected the VMs, we can verify the number of protected VMs on the Dashboard, shown in Figure 4-24.

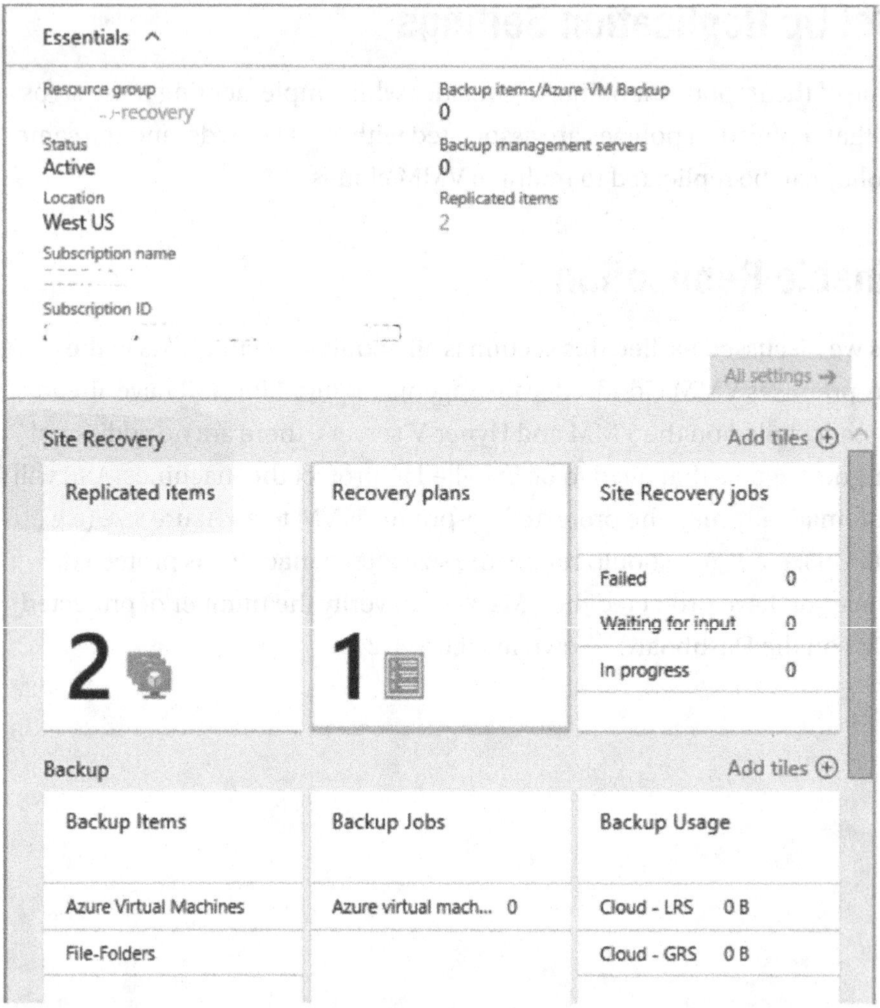

Figure 4-24. Number of Replicated VMs

Consider Configuring Failover with Network Virtualization

The ASR service provides automated replication and recovery of workloads that are configured on Hyper-V and System Center environments using Network Virtualization. This section outlines a sample configuration of Network Virtualization in VMM and the configuration of the ASR service for this environment. VMM must be configured to support VMs that will use Network Virtualization. Within the VMM console, verify whether the networking node Logical Networks is created. This is required to use Network Virtualization. Once all the necessary network configuration is done, such as network site details, IP address/VLAN, DNS, gateways, port profiles, and VM Network created, select the subnet with Isolate using Hyper-V Network Virtualization.

When the verification for the whole network configuration is satisfactory, we should be able to establish the network by configuring VMM cloud and VM settings to fail over to Azure.

The Network Virtualization settings can be verified within PowerShell by executing the following command:

```
Get-NetVirtualizationLookupRecord
```

In the output, verify the `CustomerAddress` and `ProviderAddress` fields for each VM, as shown in Figure 4-25.

```
Administrator: Windows PowerShell

PS C:\> Get-NetVirtualizationLookupRecord


CustomerAddress : 172.16.0.11
VirtualSubnetID : 2109521
MACAddress      : 001dd8b71c03
ProviderAddress : 10.1.3.10
CustomerID      : {F6365FF9-6CD3-432C-BCB3-FFCCF841994B}
Context         : SCVMM-MANAGED
Rule            : TranslationMethodEncap
VMName          : TestVM
UseVmMACAddress : False
Type            : Static

CustomerAddress : 172.16.0.1
VirtualSubnetID : 2109521
MACAddress      : 005056000000
ProviderAddress : 1.1.1.1
CustomerID      : {F6365FF9-6CD3-432C-BCB3-FFCCF841994B}
Context         : SCVMM-MANAGED
Rule            : TranslationMethodEncap
VMName          : GW
UseVmMACAddress : False
Type            : Static

CustomerAddress : 172.16.0.10
VirtualSubnetID : 2109521
MACAddress      : 001dd8b71c01
ProviderAddress : 10.1.3.10
CustomerID      : {F6365FF9-6CD3-432C-BCB3-FFCCF841994B}
Context         : SCVMM-MANAGED
Rule            : TranslationMethodEncap
VMName          : TestVM03
UseVmMACAddress : False
Type            : Static

CustomerAddress : 192.0.2.253
VirtualSubnetID : 2109521
MACAddress      : 1234567890ab
ProviderAddress : 10.1.3.10
CustomerID      : {F6365FF9-6CD3-432C-BCB3-FFCCF841994B}
Context         : SCVMM-MANAGED
Rule            : TranslationMethodEncap
VMName          : DHCPExt.sys
UseVmMACAddress : False
Type            : Static
```

Figure 4-25. Get-NetVirtualizationLookupRecord output

Scenario 3: On-Premises (VMware and Physical) to Azure

Use the following general procedures to install and configure the ASR service to protect on-premises VMs using Azure as a target location using your assigned Microsoft Azure subscription. This scenario is commonly referred to as the ASR E-to-A or enterprise-to-Azure scenario. The purpose is to become familiar with the process required to set up and configure the Microsoft Azure and VMware or physical environment to use the capabilities found within the ASR service.

Architecture

The architecture of this scenario will consist of at least one on-premises management server. There are no requirements to have Azure VMs for failover. The on-premises management server will consist of several components. The configuration server component will coordinate and manage data replication and the recovery processes. The process server acts as a replication gateway to compress, encrypt, and send replication data to Azure. The master target component handles replication data during failback from Azure. In the failback scenario, an Azure VM will be required to act as the process server (replication gateway to compress, encrypt, and send replicated data on-premises).

All management and data communication between the on-premises and Azure ASR components will be over HTTPS. There are two network replication options for replicating to Azure, either over the Internet or over an ExpressRoute public peering path (see Figure 4-26).

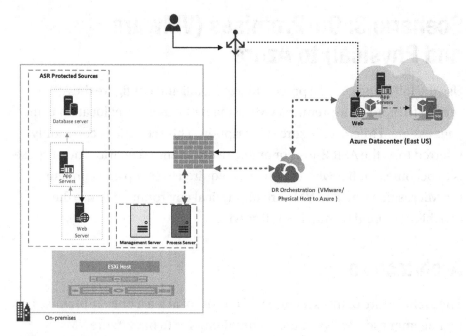

Figure 4-26. *On-premises VMware or physical server to Azure replication architecture*

Prerequisites

There are prerequisites for Azure for the on-premises management server, VMware vCenter/ESXi host(s), and protected machines.

Design Decision to Set Up Source Environment

We need to deploy an on-premises configuration server when you use the ASR service for DR of VMware VMs and physical servers to Azure (see Figure 4-27). The configuration server coordinates communications between on-premises VMware and Azure and manages data replication.

This consists of setting up the management or configuration server, registering it to the site recovery vault, adding the vCenter and administrator accounts, and connecting to vCenter (if protecting VMware VMs).

- The VMware account permissions can be found at `https://azure.microsoft.com/en-us/documentation/articles/site-recovery-vmware-to-azure/#vmware-account-permissions`.

- To deploy additional process servers (management servers only consisting of the process server component) for scalability, please follow the instructions at `https://azure.microsoft.com/en-us/documentation/articles/site-recovery-vmware-to-azure/#deploy-additional-process-servers`.

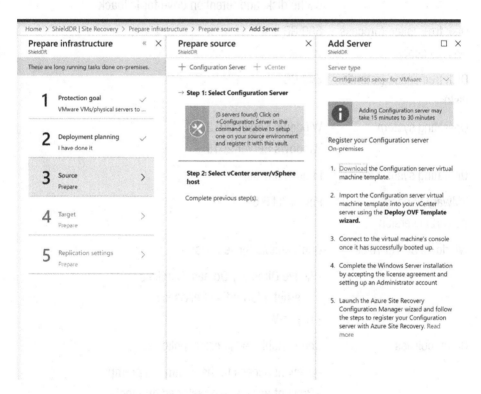

Figure 4-27. *Prepare source and target replication infrastructure for VMware or physical to Azure*

There is a brief checklist of design decisions before deploying ASR shown in Table 4-5. In addition, there are prerequisites and supported workloads for the source environment.

Table 4-5. *Design Decisions for Deploying ASR*

Design Decision	
Component	**Requirement**
CPU cores	8
RAM	12 GB
Number of disks	3, including the operating system disk, process server cache disk, and retention drive for failback
Disk free space (process server cache)	600 GB
Disk free space (retention disk)	600 GB
Operating system	Windows Server 2012 R2 Windows Server 2016
Operating system locale	English (en-us)
VMware vSphere PowerCLI version	PowerCLI 6.0
Windows Server roles	Don't enable these roles: - Active Directory Domain Services - Internet Information Services - Hyper-V
Group policies	Don't enable these group policies: - Prevent access to the command prompt - Prevent access to registry editing tools - Trust logic for file attachments - Turn on script execution

(continued)

Table 4-5. *(continued)*

	Design Decision
Component	**Requirement**
IIS	- No pre-existing default website
	- Enable Anonymous Authentication
	- Enable FastCGI setting
	- No pre-existing website/application listening on port 443
NIC type	VMXNET3 (when deployed as a VMware VM)
IP address type	Static
Internet access	The server needs access to these URLs:
	- `*.accesscontrol.windows.net`
	- `*.backup.windowsazure.com`
	- `*.store.core.windows.net`
	- `*.blob.core.windows.net`
	- `*.hypervrecoverymanager.windowsazure.com`
	- `https://cdn.mysql.com/archives/mysql-5.5/mysql-5.5.37-win32.msi` (not required for Scale-out Process Servers)
	- `time.nist.gov`
	- `time.windows.com`
Ports	443, 9443

Set Up the Target Environment

When replicating to a premium storage account, a standard storage account must also be used to store replication logs that capture ongoing changes to on-premises data (see Figure 4-28).

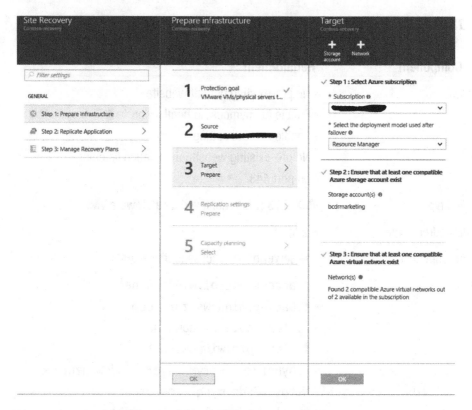

Figure 4-28. Configuring the target environment

Set Up the Replication Settings

Select the settings for the first replication policy that will be associated with the configuration server (see Figure 4-29). With ASR, you create replication policies to define specific settings that affect both RTO and RPO. With VMware, physical machines, and Azure, replication is continuous. Additionally, you must specify retention of the recovery points.

There are some notable considerations in implementing this step.

- The RPO threshold is only associated with generating alerts once the specified threshold is exceeded; it does not influence the speed of replication.

- If you do not want to use application-consistent snapshots, set it to zero.

- When using the application-consistent snapshots during a failover, the point-in-time pruning rolls up to one-hour point for every hour. For example, if you set the application-consistency snapshot to 30 minutes, ASR will take two snapshots, but will only retain the latest one for the last hour. It is better to avoid taking 15- or 30-minute snapshots and use one- to two-hour frequencies instead.

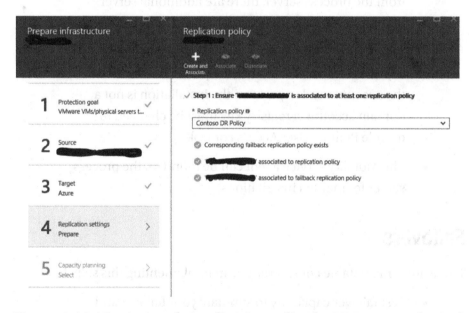

Figure 4-29. *Setting up the replication policy for VMware or physical to Azure*

Enable Replication

Now the on-premises machines can be protected and placed into protection groups by deploying the Mobility service agent. Once the agent is installed, the initial replication will begin and once completed, the continuous delta replication will begin. Also, after the initial replication is completed, the protected machine properties can be configured to the appropriate Azure VM settings during a failover. There are some notable considerations while implementing this step.

- When the Mobility service agent is push installed from the process server, there are additional server requirements for both Windows and Linux machines.

- When the Mobility service agent is push installed to a Windows machine from the process server and the account used to perform the installation is not a domain account, a registry key must be changed to disable Remote User Access control.

- The Mobility service agent can be found on the process server for manual installations.

Failovers

There are some notable considerations in implementing this step.

- Test failover capability to simulate your failover and recovery processes. This doesn't affect your source environment and regular continuous replication is uninterrupted.

- When a test failover is initiated, the disks being replicated will be cloned in the same storage account to create the temporary VMs. Because the replication will be ongoing and temporary VMs will be running at the same time, the performance impact to storage must be accounted for. For example, if you are replicating 40 disks to a single standard storage account to stay within the 20,000 IOPS limit and run a test failover for machines using all of those disks, you will likely see performance issues because the IOPS might be throttled (ASR replication of 40 disks + 40 disks for the running temporary VMs).

- There is no way for ASR to automatically initial a failover; this is by design.

- A test failover will delete the test environment after the testing has been completed when the user selects Complete Failover in the test failover job. By default, the test failover infrastructure and VMs will automatically be deleted after two weeks. This might change in the future.

- To get the best performance when you fail over to Azure, install the Azure Agent on the protected machine. It makes booting faster and helps with troubleshooting. Install the Linux or Windows agent.

- Ensure the machines are configured for remote access (e.g., SSH, RDP) so they can be managed after a failover.

Complete Prerequisites for Failback

To fail back VMware VMs and physical servers, an on-premises VMware environment is required; failing back to physical servers is not supported. A VPN or ExpressRoute circuit is required for failback. Also, a process server needs to be created in Azure and a master target server needs to be created in the on-premises VMware environment. The management server already has a master target component integrated, but you might want to create a separate master target server dedicated to failback, depending on the volume of data failing back.

There are some notable considerations in implementing this step.

- When using ExpressRoute for failback, the on-premises process server can be leveraged and a new process server does not need to be built in Azure.

- The configuration server is required on-premises for failback. In case of a disaster, the configuration server must be restored with the same IP address or the failback will not work. Ensure regular backups are taken of the configuration server.

- When failing back to an alternate location, the data will be recovered to the same data store and the same ESX host as that used by the master target server.

- When a VMware VM is failed over and now wants to be failed back to the original source, only the delta changes will be failed back.

- Failing back Windows servers requires a Windows master target server and failing back Linux servers requires a Linux master target server.

Failback Approach

To failback on-premises, the failed over Azure VMs need to be reprotected. You can fail back to the original VMware VM or you can fail back to an alternate location.

To fail back VMware machines and physical servers from Azure to on-premises, we need a failback infrastructure, which has following requirements.

- Set up a process server temporarily in Azure. We need this to act as a process server and to handle replication from Azure to on-premises. We can delete this VM after failback finishes.

- We require a VPN connection because to fail back, we need a VPN connection or ExpressRoute from the Azure network to the on-premises site.

- The master target server that was installed with the configuration server on the on-premises VMware VM handles failback. If we need to fail back large volumes of traffic, though, we then need to set up a separate on-premises master target server for this purpose.

- Verify whether the failback policy is in place to replicate back to the on-premises site and this policy is automatically created when we create a replication policy from on-premises to Azure.

  - This policy is automatically associated with the configuration server.

  - By default, policy values are RPO threshold, 15 minutes; recovery point retention, 24 hours; app-consistent snapshot frequency, 60 minutes.

- Also make sure that all the required components are deployed that are important to have in place for failback to perform. Components include a process server in Azure, an on-premises master target server, and a VPN site-to-site connection (or ExpressRoute private peering) for failback.

- Make sure you have completed the requirements for reprotection and failback. Also enable reprotection of Azure VMs, so that they are replicating from Azure to the on-premises site. This is very important because VMs must be in a replicated state to fail back to on-premises.

- All the ports must be open for reprotection and failback. Figure 4-30 and Figure 4-31, respectively, show the ports and reprotect and failback flow.

Source ▼	Destination ▼	Port ▼	Traffic (size) ▼
Protected VM	Process Server	9443	Replication (heavy)
Protected VM	Configuration Server	443	Control (light)
Process Server (on prem)	Vcenter	443	Control (light)
Process Server	Configuration Server	443	Control (light)
Master Target	Process Server	9443	Replication - optimized (heavy)
Master Target	Configuration Server	443	Control (light)

Figure 4-30. *Required reprotection and failback ports*

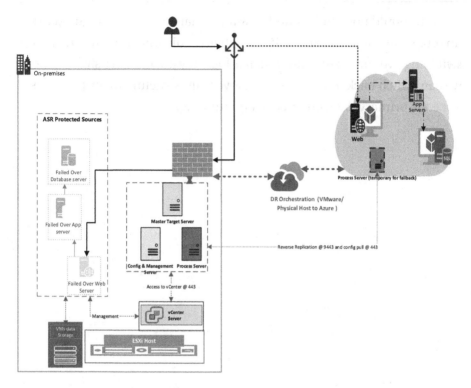

Figure 4-31. *Failback architecture from Azure to VMware or physical*

Summary

This chapter concentrated on the on-premises-to-Azure solution. We can categorize this into three scenarios: Hyper-V on-premises to Azure, Hyper-V managed by SCVMM, and finally VMware or physical on-premises-based infrastructure scenarios.

We first focused on the common best practices, prerequisites, and requirements that have to be in place for all the on-premises to Azure solutions using ASR. We also covered the architecture, planning, achievement of DR for each of the scenarios.

You should now understand how and what has to be configured to set up replication, failover, and failback activity. This will ultimately help in switching over the Azure site, which is logically a secondary site. Further, we can switch back infrastructure failover infrastructure to on-premises once the primary datacenter is up and running.

CHAPTER 5

On-Premises to On-Premises Using ASR

In this chapter we are going to focus on DR planning and configuration points we must consider while we face customer requirements to design and build a DR solution between the primary on-premises datacenter and a physical secondary datacenter in another location.

In this chapter we see how ASR is solely responsible for orchestrating and managing data DR among the primary and the secondary site. IT also acts as a communication channel between the two geographically separated physical sites.

DR Planning

The purpose of setting up DR is to be able to recover applications and continue with business activity even if the primary datacenter is experiencing an outage. ASR provides recovery plans as a construct to create the DR plan with a few important considerations to keep in mind.

© Bapi Chakraborty and Yashajeet Chowdhury 2020
B. Chakraborty and Y. Chowdhury, *Introducing Disaster Recovery with Microsoft Azure*,
https://doi.org/10.1007/978-1-4842-5917-7_5

- *Network connectivity:* Configure network mapping in ASR between the primary and secondary networks. ASR will use the mapping to connect the VM to the virtual networks on the recovery site so that application VMs can communicate to ensure application functionality.

- *Application connectivity:* As part of a DR strategy, we need to plan how an application will be accessible postfailover from the recovery site, which will help the application to be accessible to the other applications and users on an IP address or a DNS name.

- *Boot order:* Some applications need a proper order in which VMs are made available to ensure interdependency is created properly. ASR can help us to plan the boot order by placing VMs in different groups so we can prioritize and sequence which should come first, followed by dependent groups of applications. To achieve lower RTO of an application it is advisable to put VMs in the same group if they don't have dependencies between them. This will ensure that a recovery plan will parallel start these VMs during failover and hence reduce the RTO for application.

- *Application configuration:* A recovery plan provides constructs of scripts and manual steps that can be used for application configuration because in certain scenarios applications need configuration to be done after the VMs are booted up.

- *Perform DR exercise:* To ensure that a DR environment will work as expected in a disaster, it is essential to validate the strategy. Using ASR we can conduct a DR drill initially by performing test failovers that will help to create an environment similar to a production environment without affecting the DR protection or primary site impact.

Life Cycle of Existing Scenarios

The ASR scenario for replication between on-premises VMware or physical datacenters is reaching the end of its support period.

- Since August 2018, the scenario is not available in the Recovery Services Vault, and the InMage Scout software cannot be downloaded from the Vault. Figure 5-1 indicates that the on-premises to secondary recovery site options are no longer available with the VMware option that was available previously.

Protection goal
vault850

Where are your machines located? *

| On-premises | ∨ |

Where do you want to replicate your
machines to? *

| To recovery site | ∨ |

Are you performing a migration?

| Yes | ∨ |

ℹ️ We strongly recommend that you use
the new 'Azure Migrate: Server
Migration' capability to migrate
VMware, Hyper-V, and physical servers
to Azure. Click here

☑ I understand, but I would like to
continue with Azure Site Recovery

Are your machines virtualized? *

| Yes, with Hyper-V | ∧ |
| Yes, with Hyper-V | |

manage your Hyper-V hosts? *

| Yes | ∨ |

Are you managing the recovery site with
another System Center VMM? *

| Yes | ∨ |

⚠️ Note that this configuration of
replicating between Hyper-V sites will
not be supported by Azure Site
Recovery after **February 2023.** We
recommend you read our guidance
before proceeding.

☐ I have read and understood that this
configuration will not be supported after
February 2023.

Figure 5-1. *Azure Site Recovery with no more VMware as an option
for recovery configuration between sites*

- The existing deployments will be supported until
  December 31, 2020; after that, the scenario won't be
  supported.

- Existing partners can onboard new customers to the
  scenario until support ends.

Hyper-V primary site to Hyper-V secondary site is not supported
using ASR any more, as indicated in Figure 5-2. In such a scenario, the
recommendation is to use the built-in Hyper-V replica solution.

Figure 5-2. *Hyper-V to Hyper-V site recovery without SCVMM support is no longer available*

Starting in March 2020, the Azure portal began displaying notification related to the upcoming deprecation of site-to-site replication of Hyper-V VMs. The deprecation is planned to go into effect as of March 2023, as shown in Figure 5-3. If you have an existing configuration, however, it will not be affected.

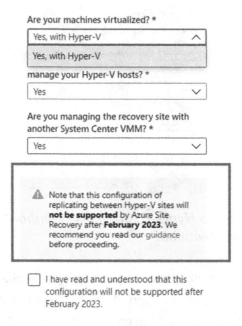

Figure 5-3. *SCVMM end of support notification using ASR for site-to-site recovery*

When any of these scenarios are deprecated, the existing replications might get disrupted and customers will not be able to view, manage, or performs any DR-related operations via ASR. There are several alternate options from which to choose.

- As recommended by Microsoft, we should start considering using Azure as the DR target.

- Use the built-in Hyper-V replica solution to continue site-to-site replication. However, this has a limitation in regard to managing the DR configurations, which we get as a single-pane advantage while using ASR through the Azure portal.

Scenario 4: Hyper-V-to-Hyper-V with VMM

In Chapter 4 we discussed the scenarios where ASR can be used for planning and setting up a DR solution from on-premises to Azure whether it is from Hyper-V or VMware or a physical environment to Azure, and even in the case of protecting an Azure IaaS infrastructure within Azure. Now let us explore what will happen when we have to plan and establish a DR solution between customer-owned sites managed by SCVMM using ASR. This scenario describes how to replicate on-premises Hyper-V VMs managed in SCVMM clouds to Azure, using ASR in the Azure portal.

Planning and Prerequisites

You should ensure that architectural components are in place such as an Azure subscription, VMM server, Hyper-V server, and Hyper-V VMs. There are a few common steps as covered in the scenarios in Chapter 4.

1. Create a Recovery Services Vault.

2. Choose a protection goal. The difference here is to select To Recovery Site as the protection goal.

3. Install the Azure Site Recovery Provider. In this scenario we must run the Provider setup file on each VMM server as referenced in Figure 5-4.

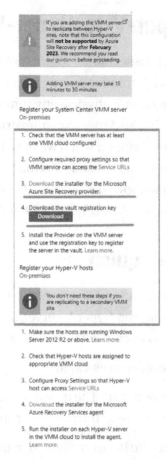

Figure 5-4. Option to download Microsoft Azure Site Recovery Provider and the Recovery Services Vault registration key

4.   Set up the target environment. Here you should select the private cloud that you want to replicate to the secondary site (see Figure 5-5).

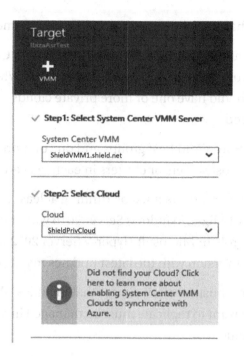

Figure 5-5. *Setting up the target environment*

5. Set up a replication policy. In configuring the
    replication policy for this scenario, we must follow
    a few best practices by selecting the correct options
    for settings like Hyper-V host version, authentication
    type, authentication port, copy frequency, recovery
    point retention, data transfer compression,
    app-consistent snapshot frequency, and initial
    replication method.

6. Finally, enable replication.

This scenario has the following on-premises requirements.

- One or more VMM servers running on System Center 2012 R2 or the latest supported version. Each VMM server should have one or more private clouds configured.

- One or more VMM host groups and one or more Hyper-V host servers or clusters in each host group.

- Hyper-V host servers must be running at least Windows Server 2012 R2 or Windows Server 2016 with the Hyper-V role or Microsoft Hyper-V Server 2012 R2 or the latest version with the latest updates installed.

- A Hyper-V host server or cluster that includes VMs that you want to replicate must be managed in a VMM cloud.

- Make sure that VMM servers and Hyper-V hosts comply with the support matrix as per Microsoft's suggested standards.

- Make sure that you don't have any UEFI/ EFI boot, because it is not supported.

- Make sure that guest operating system is as suggested for Hyper-V on Windows Server 2016 or Windows Server 2012 R2 as per Microsoft standard support.

- Remember that guest VM NIC teaming is not supported. If the source VM has NIC teaming, it is converted to a single NIC after failover to Azure.

The final bit of planning is to prepare VMM servers for network mapping.

Architecture and Concepts

This scenario is possible as Hyper-V Manager and ASR use Hyper-V Replica to migrate the VMs between sites. Figure 5-6 provides a basic understanding of the customer DR architecture of an SCVMM-based infrastructure using ASR between the two physical sites.

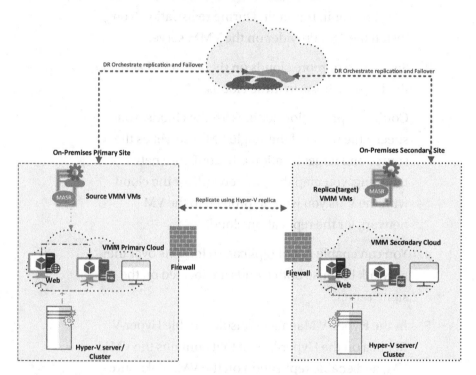

Figure 5-6. *Primary site to secondary site (recovery site) with SCVMM architecture*

Create Recovery Services Vault

The steps to configure the Recovery Services Vault are nearly same as outlined in Chapter 4 for other scenarios.

1. Create a Recovery Services Vault, generate and download a vault registration key, and register the VMM server in the vault. During registration, you install the ASR Provider on the VMM server.

2. Set up one or more clouds on the VMM VM and add the Hyper-V hosts to these clouds.

3. Configure protection settings for the clouds. You specify the name of the single VMM server as the source and target locations. To configure network mapping, you map the VM network for the cloud with the VMs you want to protect, to the VM network for the replication cloud.

4. You can enable initial replication for VMs over the network because both clouds are located on the same server.

5. In the Hyper-V Manager console, enable Hyper-V Replica on the Hyper-V host that contains the VMM VM, and enable replication on the VM. Make sure you don't add the VMM VM to any clouds that are protected by ASR. This ensures that Hyper-V Replica settings aren't overridden by ASR.

If you want to create recovery plans, you specify the same VMM server for source and target.

Plan, Design, and Execute the Network

Network Mapping

We must plan and execute the network mapping between on-premises VMM VM networks in the source and secondary site, which will help in connecting the VMs to the correct targeted VMs on the secondary site. That also helps optimize the replication between the Hyper-V host servers. If you don't configure network mapping, replica VMs won't be connected to a VM network after failover.

First we have to prepare the VMM infrastructure.

1. Configure the VMM logical network for both the primary and secondary VMM infrastructure servers associated with the respective private cloud.

2. Configure the VM networks and make sure they are linked to the logical network in each location.

3. Connect VMs on the source Hyper-V hosts to the source VM network.

Network mapping works as follows.

- Network mapping can be configured on a single VMM server if two sites are managed by the same server or between VM networks on two VMM servers.

- Replication will be enabled properly and when mapping is configured correctly, a VM at the primary location will be connected to a network, and its replica at the target location will be connected to its mapped network.

- When we select the target VM network during network mapping in ASR, the VMM source clouds that use the source VM network will be displayed, along with the available target VM networks on the target clouds that are used for protection.

- If the target network has multiple subnets and any of
  these subnets has the same name as the subnet on
  which the source VM is located, then the replica VM
  will be connected to that target subnet after failover. If
  there is no target subnet with a matching name, the VM
  will be connected to the first subnet in the network.

Plan Your IP Addressing

After you fail over Hyper-V VMs in SCVMM clouds to a secondary site, you
need to be able connect to the replica VMs. You can achieve this in two
ways.

- *Retain the same IP address after failover:* When we
  need to maintain the same IP address as the primary
  VM when failover will happen to a secondary site,
  this option will solve the network-related issues after
  failover. To achieve this we can select one of two
  methods.

  - Deploy a stretched subnet between the primary
    and the secondary sites.

  - Perform a full subnet failover from the primary to
    the secondary site. You need to update routes to
    indicate the new location of the IP addresses.

- *Use a different IP address after failover:* This scenario is
  perfect when it is okay with the application architecture
  if the VM gets a new IP address after failover. We must
  understand, however, that we might have to make
  necessary DNS record updates in place in this scenario.

Monitoring

Monitoring systems are a critical piece of all datacenter solutions. In a DR solution, monitoring systems help you track the ongoing health of the system and DR operations. You can use the process enumerated next to set up monitoring with ASR.

Setting Up Monitoring Infrastructure

ASR monitoring can be viewed in two parts: operational monitoring and steady-state monitoring.

- As part of configuring the protection or performing DR actions, various jobs are triggered. The progress and success of these jobs can be monitored using the ASR Azure portal or the ASR APIs. You can also download the job results to create compliance reports. To monitor health, go to Jobs view, which gives the status of all jobs.

- You can also configure the ASR vault to send email notifications. This allows you to easily monitor replication health and receive notifications if there is a replication error, network connectivity failure, and so on.

- The most critical part of a DR solution is to know when the system replication is getting affected.

Debugging and Troubleshooting

If you are not able to rectify an issue with the help of monitoring systems and help messages, you can also reach out to Microsoft support for help with the issue. To help collect the right information to help Microsoft debug the issues, use the integrated log collector to report the issue to

Microsoft Support. You need to enable the tool settings and rerun the ASR scenario that is not working as appropriate. Figure 5-7 shows the SCVMM Troubleshooter.

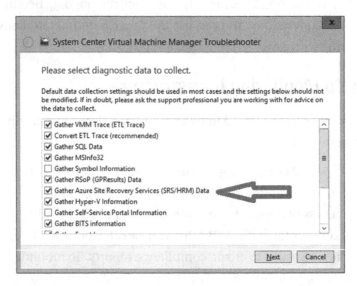

Figure 5-7. *The SCVMM Troubleshooter*

Scenario 5: Replicate On-Premises VMware Virtual Machines or Physical Servers to a Secondary Site

ASR uses the InMage Scout application, which provides replication between VMware sites or between a physical server and a secondary site. Because this scenario is no longer available to configure for any new on-premises primary site to secondary site replication solution, we are covering the architecture components only.

Architecture and Concepts

There are four main components for this scenario.

1. *Configuration server:* This is an on-premises machine that coordinates communication and manages the data replication and recovery processes. You run Unified Setup on this machine to install the configuration server and these additional components:

    - *Process server:* This acts as a replication gateway. It receives replication data from protected source machines; optimizes it with caching, compression, and encryption; and sends it to Azure Storage. It also handles push installation of the Mobility service to protected machines and performs automatic discovery of VMware VMs. The default process server is installed on the configuration server. You can deploy additional stand-alone process servers to scale your deployment.

2. *Master target server:* This server handles replication data during failback from Azure.

3. *Mobility service:* This component is deployed on every machine (VMware VM or physical server) that you want to replicate to Azure. It captures data writes on the machine and forwards them to the process server.

    - *Azure:* You don't need to create any Azure VMs to handle replication and failover to Azure. You do need an Azure subscription, an Azure Storage account to store replicated data, and an Azure virtual network for Azure VMs to connect to after failover. The Storage account and network must be in the same region as the Recovery Services Vault.

4. *Failback:* You need several components for failback:

- *Temporary process server:* You need an Azure VM as a temporary process server. You can delete it after failback is complete.

- *VPN:* You need a VPN (or Azure ExpressRoute) connection between your on-premises site and the Azure network in which your Azure VMs are located.

- *Master target server:* If failback traffic is heavy, you might need to set up a dedicated master target server machine on-premises. For lighter traffic, the default master target server running on the configuration server can be used.

Summary

In this chapter we discussed currently supported site-to-site DR approaches using ASR. We looked in depth at Hyper-V-to-Hyper-V with SCVMM in the context of important factors we must consider at the time of planning, prerequisites, and what major components we need to implement in the course of enabling an Azure environment. We also covered the important changes and deprecation before selecting a scenario approach.

CHAPTER 6

Application High Availability and Disaster Recovery on Azure

In our previous chapters we learned about various DR scenarios, architectural constructs, considerations, and design principles. Although these architectural constructs and design considerations apply to most of the applications and situations, there are a few special cases requiring different design and implementation. Such applications are those enterprise applications that implement their own methods of DR. This is solely due to how they are designed, coded, and structured to ensure functionality and data consistency.

In this chapter we explore Microsoft Windows Server Active Directory, SQL Server, Systems Applications and Products (SAP), and Remote Desktop Services and learn how to design recovery solutions for them on Microsoft Azure. We will also look at the inherent recovery capabilities of such applications and what additional considerations must be kept in mind. Please note that this is not a comprehensive list and you should identify whether such applications exist in your portfolio while designing a DR plan.

© Bapi Chakraborty and Yashajeet Chowdhury 2020
B. Chakraborty and Y. Chowdhury, *Introducing Disaster Recovery with Microsoft Azure*,
https://doi.org/10.1007/978-1-4842-5917-7_6

Windows Active Directory Disaster Recovery on Azure

Microsoft Windows Server Active Directory is a critical service that exists in almost all enterprises. This is a key identity, authentication, and authorization service that serves applications, users, and devices. Any failure or inconsistency in the Active Directory database can lead to application failures, exceptions, negative user experiences, or entire infrastructure outages. Active Directory implements its own multimaster replication and keeps all domain controllers (DCs) in an enterprise in sync. This creates two scenarios from a DR perspective.

1. Include recovery of the Active Directory service as part of the application recovery (if it depends on Active Directory). Alternatively, ensure that there is already an existing Active Directory infrastructure in the recovery site for the application. This is required for situations wherein we have applications hosted on Azure or on-premises that depend on on-premises Active Directory.

2. DR planning for the Active Directory service includes keeping multiple DCs in each site or physical location. It is also important for good backups to be available to perform authoritative or nonauthoritative modes of restoration of the service if needed.

In this section, we discuss how we can extend the Active Directory Directory Service infrastructure to Azure for the purpose of application recovery. Approaches include:

*   Extend on-premises Active Directory to Azure (IaaS). This is the and recommended practice.

*   Use ASR for Active Directory Directory Service.

Extend On-Premises Active Directory Infrastructure to Azure (IaaS)

Nearly all applications depend on Active Directory and DNS infrastructure for authentication, authorization, and name resolution. There are several factors that control how a DC should be replicated to the recovery site. In such cases we need to extend the on-premises Active Directory environment to the recovery site (e.g., Azure) by introducing a new VM(s) as DC. Before that, however, we must address a few preliminary considerations.

- Gather necessary application dependency and Active Directory architecture details such as Active Directory forest, domain and domain controllers, Flexible Single Master Operation (FSMO) roles, and any other application services that are hosted on the DCs.

- Gather existing Azure subscription and network configuration details such as firewall ports, routing, and so on.

- Follow the necessary prerequisites for hosting a DC on Azure. You can read more about various aspects of this on the Microsoft documentation site at `https://docs.microsoft.com/en-us/azure/architecture/reference-architectures/identity/adds-extend-domain`.

It is recommended that whenever there is more than one DC in an environment, you use Active Directory replication to replicate the DC to the recovery site. Also, if you ever intend to fail over a partial site, it is recommended that you use Active Directory replication and keep active DCs on both the sites.

The following are the high-level steps that need to be implemented.

1. Create a virtual network with a proper dedicated subnet for Identity and Access Management (IAM) infrastructure to be placed.

2. Create a VM and associate it to the dedicated subnet for IAM.

3. Make sure the network connectivity has already been established between the on-premises and Azure virtual network (vNet) using a site-to-site VPN or ExpressRoute.

4. Add the on-premises Active Directory DNS address in Azure vNet as custom DNS.

5. On-premises, create a site to represent the region where you created an Azure virtual network by using Active Directory Sites and Services.

6. Join the newly created VM into the existing on-premises domain.

7. Install Active Directory Domain Services in the Azure VM that we created for a dedicated new DC role server in Azure and promote the server as the DC in the existing domain.

8. Reconfigure DNS Server for the virtual network to include the Azure DC. Figure 6-1 depicts the DNS configuration page for Virtual Network vNet_Contoso. In this image, the IP address of the DC which is also the DNS server in Azure VM is 10.3.0.4. All existing systems in the virtual network will require a reboot to discover and use the new DNS server on Azure, which is also an Active Directory server. All new deployments of VMs will discover it automatically.

Figure 6-1. *Custom DNS configuration page for Azure Virtual Network*

Note   We can configure the Active Directory infrastructure with a delayed replication interval that allows a time window during which invalid or improper changes to Active Directory can be rolled back through the "authoritative restore" process. This can be done by modifying the Replicate Every value from 180 minutes to a higher value such as 1,440 minutes by using the Active Directory Sites and Services connection.

Use Azure Site Recovery for Domain Controller Replication

ASR is application agnostic and it replicates a VM as an object in a crash-consistent state. We can use ASR to create a DR plan for an Active Directory environment so that when disaster strikes, we can initiate a failover to bring up the Active Directory server (DC) and get it running in a few minutes. While failing over a single or multiple applications using ASR, ensure that you fail over Active Directory first or bring up the DC first in the recovery site before any other application or database servers.

Planning Guidance

To replicate a DC using ASR, consider the following information.

- Your Azure subscription is configured with an Azure virtual network, a Storage account, and a Recovery Services Vault before planning the replication onto Azure. Refer to Chapters 4 and 5 for a support matrix for on-premises and Azure VMs.

- The required accounts for managing Azure and domain admins for all domains are in place.

- On-premises domains should have full network connectivity to Azure vNet.

- All security and compliance requirements must be met, such as firewall ports being allowed for replication.

- In an environment that has several DCs and distributed FSMO roles, prefer a DC that is:

    - A global catalog server and a DNS server.

    - The FSMO role owner for roles that are needed after a test failover. Otherwise, these roles will need to be seized after the failover.

- In the case of multiple DCs in the environment, set up an additional DC on the target recovery site.

- For the replicated VM network configuration, configure Site Recovery settings to ensure that the VM is attached to the correct network after failover.

- Make sure the DNS changes have been added to a specific targeted vNet.

- You must consider running a test failover on an isolated network to avoid any impact on production workloads.

SQL High Availability and Disaster Recovery on Azure

Another common scenario to provide an HA and DR application scenario is related to Microsoft SQL Server infrastructure. We must understand the different approaches that involve the SQL infrastructure in establishing HA and DR, and how we should plan solutions that can successfully protect data and services. The sections that follow include the solution approaches we can adopt while planning the HA and DR for SQL, depending on the scenario.

AlwaysOn Failover Cluster Instance

This approach is powered by Windows Server Failover Clustering, and then we can have the SQL Server instance installed across nodes in a cluster with shared disk storage. An AlwaysOn Failover Cluster requires shared disk storage and it can leverage AlwaysOn Availability Groups for remote DR. While configuring this approach with the latest Windows Advanced Clustering feature in place, we have different ways available to provide shared storage.

- With storage supported by a third-party clustering solution.

- With remote iSCSI target shared block storage.

- The Windows Server software-defined storage solution. We can provide attached storage using Windows Server 2016 Storage Spaces Direct (S2D).

- Using Premium File Share of the Azure Storage solution, which are SSD-backed (Solid State Drive) consistently low-latency file shares that are fully supported for use with Failover Cluster Instance.

AlwaysOn Availability Group

We can have an HA solution for SQL Server at a database level with AlwaysOn Availability Groups (AGs). We can also create an HA solution at an instance level with AlwaysOn Failover Cluster Instances. For additional redundancy, we can further create redundancy at both levels by creating AGs on failover cluster instances. We need to have Active Directory Domain Service, because Windows failover clustering requires an Active Directory domain.

The advanced features of AGs can support a set of primary databases and one to eight sets of corresponding secondary databases. In this case, each replica resides on a separate instance of SQL Server and on individual physical nodes or cloud-based VMs. There is no need for shared storage.

Note   AG listeners are supported on Azure VMs running Windows Server 2008 R2, Windows Server 2012, Windows Server 2012 R2, and Windows Server 2016. This is possible using load-balanced endpoints enabled on the Azure VMs that are AG nodes.

As showcased in Figure 6-2, a simple architecture of an on-premises SQL AG is extended to Azure by adding a new SQL node. In this scenario we must keep some planning considerations in place.

- You must have extended the domain onto Azure by placing an additional DC at the Azure site for a successful operational DR environment of your databases.

- You must make sure that all availability replicas are in the same failover cluster.

- The cluster must span both networks (a multisubnet failover cluster). This configuration requires a VPN or ExpressRoute connectivity between Azure and the on-premises network.

- We can also use the Add Replica Wizard in SQL Server Management Studio (SSMS) to add an Azure replica to an existing AlwaysOn AG.

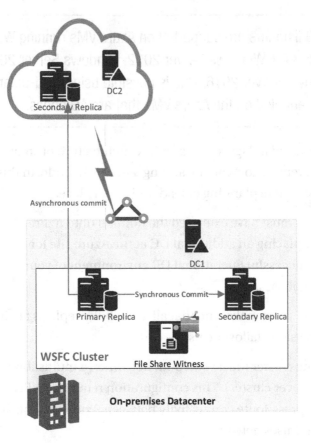

Figure 6-2. *Extending on-premises SQL Server Availability Group by adding a secondary node on Azure*

Database Mirroring

This approach provides HA and protection for a single database, with one mirror allowed per database; for reference see Figure 6-3. It maintains two copies of a single database that reside in different instances of SQL Server. In many customer scenarios it is implemented and spread across different datacenters or geographical locations to protect against failures. In this approach, the secondary database always acts as a warm standby server and takes over the moment the primary goes down. Mirroring supports failover with zero loss of data via a witness server, which is a separate Microsoft SQL Server that monitors the primary instance, and ensures a smooth switchover in the event of a failure. We can configure this in either High-Safety mode or High-Performance mode. High-Safety mode makes sure the data is always exactly the same in both databases, with transactions being written to both databases at the same time.

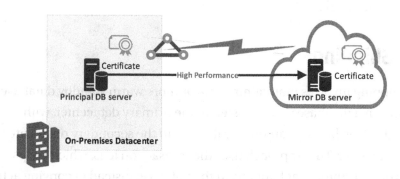

Figure 6-3. *Basic on-premises to Azure database mirroring architecture*

Microsoft is phasing out database mirroring in future versions of SQL Server, replacing it with Basic Availability Groups.

Note   SQL Server database mirroring is not supported for SQL Server 2008 or SQL Server 2008 R2 on an Azure VM.

When we plan to extend the mirroring approach to cloud, we must ensure the following conditions.

- One mirroring partner VM running in Azure and the other running on-premises for cross-site DR using server certificates. Partners do not need to be in the same Active Directory domain, and no VPN connection is required.

- We can also have another mirroring scenario that involves one partner running in an Azure VM and the other running on-premises in the same Active Directory domain for cross-site DR, but in this case we must have a VPN or ExpressRoute connection between the Azure virtual network and the on-premises network.

Log Shipping

Log shipping involves maintaining one or more warm standby databases running on a database server hosted in the primary datacenter, with transaction log backups automatically sent to the secondary datacenter database server. This approach uses the transaction logs, which keeps tracks of everything that happens in the database instead of copying actual database objects like tables, stored procedures, and so on. It then ships everything over and writes it to the secondary SQL database servers. As a best practice, we must schedule the shipping intervals to maintain the RPO and RTO required by the client.

In an SQL log shipping scenario, when extending this to the cloud, one server should be running in Azure VM and the other running on-premises for a cross-site DR solution (see Figure 6-4). Log shipping depends on Windows file sharing, so either a VPN connection or ExpressRoute connectivity between the Azure virtual network and the on-premises network is required.

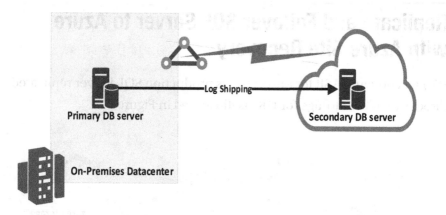

Figure 6-4. *Basic on-premises to Azure database log shipping architecture*

Azure Backup and Restore

The Azure backup solution covers all SQL Server instances with the Microsoft SQL Server Backup to Azure. We can provide a low-cost backup solution with additional storage through geo-replication along with scalable, security-enhanced, compression; auto-encryption; and the cost-effective feature of Azure Blob storage, shown in Figure 6-5.

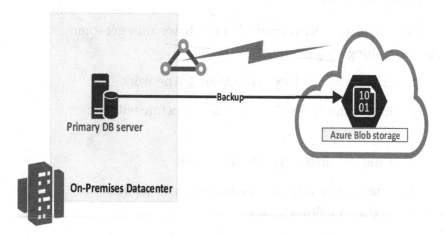

Figure 6-5. *Backup and restore example on-premises database to Azure Blob storage*

Replicate and Failover SQL Server to Azure with Azure Site Recovery

We can configure ASR for on-premises production SQL Server replicated directly to Azure Storage for DR, as illustrated in Figure 6-6.

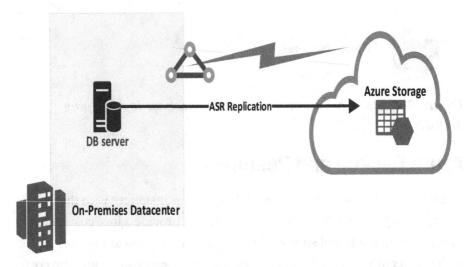

Figure 6-6. *Simple diagram for on-premises database replication to Azure storage using ASR*

Before we plan for this approach, though, we must get some preliminary things implemented.

1. Ensure connectivity to the Azure DR network.

2. Extend the Active Directory infrastructure onto the cloud.

3. Extend connectivity with other tiers.

4. Interoperate with AlwaysOn, active geo-replication, and auto-failover groups.

5. Set up on-premises to Azure using ASR.

Set Up ASR for SQL

ASR doesn't support guest clusters when replicating to an Azure region, so for this scenario the recommended approach is to protect the Microsoft SQL Server cluster to a stand-alone SQL Server instance in the primary datacenter and then recover it in the secondary datacenter, which is Azure in this scenario. To accomplish this, following these steps.

1. Configure an additional stand-alone SQL Server instance in the primary on-premises datacenter, or if the scenario involves the cluster on Azure, then set up the additional stand-alone server in the same Azure region.

2. Configure the SQL instance to serve as a mirror for the databases you want to protect and configure mirroring in High-Safety mode.

3. Configure ASR on the primary site for Azure.

4. Use Site Recovery replication to replicate the new SQL Server instance to the secondary site, which is Azure. As it is a High-Safety mirror copy, it will be synchronized with the primary cluster but replicated using ASR replication.

Failback Considerations

In the case of failback, we must understand that for SQL Server standard clusters, it requires a SQL Server backup and restore. This operation can be performed from the mirror instance to the original cluster with re-establishment of the Microsoft SQL Server database mirror.

Azure Multiregion SQL Server

If the customer has a requirement to set up an Azure multiregion application with Microsoft SQL as a back-end database to provide an HA and DR environment, we can take the architecture approach showcased in Figure 6-7. This architecture can help to achieve the DR site if an individual subsystem of the application fails. In this architecture, we can see that we have the primary application infrastructure with SQL Server as a back-end database in the Azure primary region and we have a similar setup in the Azure secondary region, which provides us a highly available application infrastructure, along with a proper DR solution constructed in the context of the database by stretching the SQL Server AlwaysOn between the nodes placed across the regions with asynchronous replication. In this scenario, if a regional outage affects the primary Azure region, we can use Traffic Manager to fail over to the secondary Azure region.

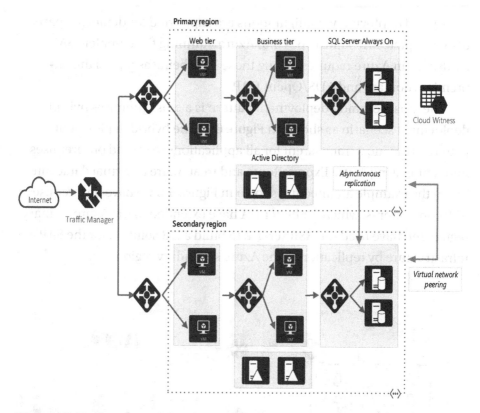

Figure 6-7. *Azure multiregion SQL server HA and DR architecture*

SAP Extension in Azure and Disaster Recovery

Azure allows enterprises to deploy applications like SAP (NetWeaver, HANA) and extend their reliability and availability parallel to the on-premises environment to avoid the resource crunch in the physical site. By establishing cross-premises connectivity, we can enable companies to actively integrate Azure VMs into their on-premises domains and their SAP system landscape. We focus on the planning and implementation considerations for SAP NetWeaver HA and DR on Azure.

Hybrid deployment configurations are supported for deploying parts of or complete SAP landscapes into Azure. Running the complete SAP landscape in Azure requires having those VMs being as part of the on-premises domain and ADS/OpenLDAP.

The most common deployment pattern is a cross-premises hybrid deployment scenario as shown in Figure 6-8. The hybrid deployment pattern is the most transparent for all applications to extend on-premises into Azure using Azure ExpressRoute and treat Azure as virtual datacenter.

In the example architecture shown in Figure 6-8 we have on-premises SAP components, which for better HA have extended to the Azure primary region and have used the ASR service to build a DR solution for the SAP infrastructure by replication to the Azure secondary region.

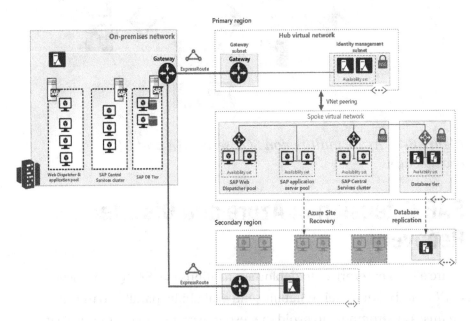

Figure 6-8. *SAP infrastructure reference architecture includes high availability by extending to Azure and disaster recovery using ASR*

In the case of SAP, each tier uses a different strategy to provide HA and DR protection. Before the design and implementation of the SAP infrastructure on the cloud, we must understand each of the roles.

- *SAP Web Dispatcher pools:* The Web Dispatcher component works as a load balancer for SAP traffic among the SAP application servers. To achieve HA for the Web Dispatcher component, Azure Load Balancer implements the parallel Web Dispatcher setup.

- *SAP Central Services clusters:* To implement an HA solution, you can use either a shared disk cluster or a file share cluster. To configure VMs for a shared disk cluster, use Windows Server Failover Cluster. We recommend that you use the cloud witness as a quorum witness.

- *SAP application server pools:* SAP Logon Groups (SMLG) transaction manages login groups for Advanced Business Application Programming (ABAP) application servers. When a user tries to log on using an SAP login then the log on program asks the message server which servers are available or active (SMLG) and then logs the user on to the best performing application server. It uses the load-balancing function within the message server of the Central Services to distribute workload among SAP application server pools for SAP GUIs and Remote Function Call (RFC) traffic. You can replicate this management using Site Recovery.

Planning SAP to Extend Infrastructure (Hybrid Model) with DR

When planning for SAP systems within one SAP landscape, the core need is to establish the communication of the SAP components and role servers with each other and with many other software components deployed across the organization, independent of their deployment form. These conditions can only be met when we have the on-premises Active Directory/OpenLDAP and DNS services extended to the Azure systems through ExpressRoute (which is the recommended network type) or site-to-site/multisite connectivity. It is important to gather the following information for planning the deployment of SAP into Azure.

- Check the SAP products supported to run in Azure as VMs. SAP has a list of certified Azure VM types such as M64ms, M128ms, and so on. While planning for SAP infrastructure on Azure we must consider that.

- Review and verify the list of operating systems that are supported with specific Azure VMs for SAP products.

- Check the database management systems that are supported for your SAP products with specific Azure VMs.

- Evaluate whether we need to move or upgrade to different operating systems as per the SAP standard guidance to deploy on Azure.

- The on-premises Active Directory/OpenLDAP/DNS has been extended via VPN or ExpressRoute as a dedicated private connection to Azure.

Networking Consideration

We must plan and select the right networking approach to map the required scenarios to set up the SAP infrastructure for the hybrid model. A few of the common required capabilities are as follows.

- Access to specific services and ports needed by applications within the VMs.

- Internal communication and name resolution between a group of VMs deployed as Azure VMs.

- Hybrid connectivity between the customer's on-premises network and the Azure network.

- Cross-region or datacenter connectivity between Azure sites in case of planning for setting up the DR site on Azure.

- Use of secure communication protocols such as SSL/TLS for browser access.

- VPN-based connections for system access to the Azure services.

- For better security, open only required ports. When deploying VMs in Azure, create an NSG to define access rules.

- Establish connectivity between the Azure Region A and Azure DR Region B.

Table 6-1 provides list of specific ports needed for SAP communication.

Table 6-1. *SAP Required Ports*

Service	Port Name	Default Range (Minimum–Maximum)	Purpose
Dispatcher	sapdp	3200–3299	SAP Dispatcher, used by SAP GUI for Windows and Java
Message server	sapms	Free	SAP-System-ID
Gateway	sapgw	Free	SAP gateway, used for Common Programming Interface for Communication (CPIC) and RFC communication
SAP router	sapdp99	Free	Only CI (central instance) Service names can be reassigned in /etc/services to an arbitrary value after installation.

Protect SAP Landscape with Azure Site Recovery

To build a cold standby site with ongoing database replication might be too expensive, especially for smaller organizations, but with ASR we can now achieve that. We can improve the DR process by implementing ASR, which replicates SAP infrastructure hosted on Azure Region A to Azure Region B and by creating a recovery plan so that we can provision resources in the cloud in case of an unexpected event.

Table 6-2 lists recommendations for DR of each tier used in this example.

Table 6-2. *Disaster Recovery Recommendations*

SAP Tiers	Recommendation
SAP Web Dispatcher pool	Replicate by using Site Recovery
SAP Application Server pool	Replicate by using Site Recovery
SAP Central Services cluster	Replicate by using Site Recovery
Active Directory virtual machines	Use Active Directory replication
SQL Database servers	Use SQL Server AlwaysOn replication

Components of SAP and DR Consideration

We need to consider different connectivity options depending on the number of users and required bandwidth. We can choose between a secured VPN or ExpressRoute connection. Apart from the type of network consideration, we also need to plan, design, and configure the following components.

- Design a recovery network.

- Replicate a DC.

- Replicate VMs.

- Replicate the database tier.

- Create a recovery plan.

  - Add VMs to failover groups. Add the Application Server, Web Dispatcher, and SAP Central Services VMs in the recovery plan and then customize to group the VMs.

  - Add scripts to the recovery plan. Update the DNS entry, change bindings and connections, and postfailover operations by adding scripts to the recovery plan.

- Test failover planning.

- Perform planned a failover.

Supported Scenarios

There are several supported scenarios to implement a DR solution using ASR for SAP application infrastructure.

- A customer has SAP systems running in one Azure datacenter, and we want to replicate them to another Azure datacenter (Azure-to-Azure DR).

- A customer has SAP systems running on VMware (or physical) servers on-premises so we are going to also replicate the SAP systems to a DR site in an Azure datacenter (VMware-to-Azure DR).

- A customer havs SAP systems running on Hyper-V on-premises and we need to replicate the SAP systems to a DR site in an Azure datacenter (Hyper-V-to-Azure DR).

Remote Desktop Services

Remote Desktop Services (RDS) provides a virtual desktop infrastructure (VDI) and session-based desktops that allow users to work anywhere.

With RDS, users can access a Remote Desktop server from within a corporate network or from the Internet. RDS lets you efficiently deploy and maintain software in an enterprise environment. You can easily deploy programs from a central location. Because you install the programs on the Remote Desktop server and not on the client computer, programs are easier to upgrade and to maintain.

When a user accesses a program on a Remote Desktop server, program execution occurs on the server. Only the keyboard, mouse, and display information are transmitted over the network. Each user sees only her own individual session. The session is managed transparently by the server operating system and is independent of any other client session.

RDS is a server role that consists of several subcomponents, known as role services in Windows Server 2008 and above.

Before jumping into an RDS DR solution, we must understand the major components of RDS. RDS consists of the role services illustrated in Figure 6-9.

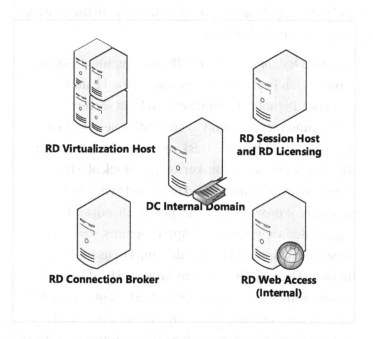

Figure 6-9. *Remote Desktop Services role components architecture*

- *Remote Desktop Virtualization Host:* The Remote Desktop Virtualization Host component integrates with Hyper-V and provides VMs that can be used as either personal virtual desktops or virtual desktop pools.

- *Remote Desktop Session Host:* The Remote Desktop Session Host role service enables a server to host Windows-based programs or the full Windows desktop. End users connect to the Remote Desktop Session Host server via Remote Desktop Connection Broker or RemoteApp to access session-based desktops and published applications, to save files, and to use network resources on that server.

- *Remote Desktop Connection Broker:* Remote Desktop Connection Broker supports session load balancing between Remote Dekstop Session Host servers in a farm and reconnection to an existing session in a load-balanced Remote Desktop server farm. Remote Desktop Connection Broker keeps a track of which is where, who to talk to, and what to do with RDS requests. It provides a single, personalized, and aggregated view of RemoteApp programs, session-based desktops, and virtual desktops to users. Using Remote Desktop Connection Broker to load balance sessions involves two phases. In the first phase, initial connections are distributed by a preliminary load-balancing mechanism, such as DNS round robin. After a user authenticates, the Remote Desktop Session Host server that accepted the initial connection queries the Remote Desktop Connection Broker server to determine where to redirect the user.

- *Remote Desktop Web Access:* Remote Desktop Web
  Access provides users with a customizable web
  portal for accessing session-based desktops, virtual
  desktops, and RemoteApp programs. It enables users
  to access RemoteApp programs and a Remote Desktop
  connection to the Remote Desktop Session Host server
  through a website. Remote Desktop Web Access also
  includes Remote Desktop Web Connection, which
  enables users to remotely connect to any computer
  where they have Remote Desktop access.

- *Remote Desktop Licensing:* Remote Desktop Licensing
  manages the Remote Desktop client access licenses
  (CALs) that are required for each device or user to
  connect to a Remote Desktop server. You use Remote
  Desktop Licensing to install, issue, and monitor the
  availability of Remote Desktop CALs on a Remote
  Desktop license server. There are two types of Terminal
  Services CALs:

  - Remote Desktop Per Device CALs

  - Remote Desktop Per User CALs

- *Remote Desktop Gateway:* Remote Desktop Gateway
  enables authorized remote users to connect to
  resources on an internal corporate network from any
  Internet-connected device that can run the Remote
  Desktop Connection client. It also enables compatible
  devices to securely connect over the Internet to Remote
  Desktop Session Host servers or Remote Desktop
  Virtualization Host servers behind a corporate firewall.
  Remote Dektop Gateway is to be placed at the edge of a

corporate network to filter out incoming RDS requests
by referencing criteria defined in a designated network
policy server (NPS). With a server certificate, Remote
Dekstop Gateway offers secure remote access to RDS
infrastructure.

With the new RDS solution, we can expand our RDS environment
as a hybrid solution. We can deploy RDS with Azure services to reduce
infrastructure maintenance costs for on-premises servers, increase
stability by using Azure services to ensure HA, improve security by using
multifactor authentication, and improve users' experience by using
existing identities to access resources in RDS. The following are the
availability options for the solution by solution component.

- *RD Session Broker:* The only option for increasing
  availability of RD Session Broker is Windows
  Clustering.

- *RD Session Host:* Availability is ensured by grouping
  servers with same applications into RD farms.

- *RD Web Access:* Availability can be increased by adding
  another server and configuring an NLB cluster. We can
  even have the Azure Active Directory Application Proxy
  connector implemented on RD Web and can integrate
  it with Azure Active Directory.

In planning for RDS with ASR for DR, we should understand what we
can replicate, and there are two scenarios.

- Replicate managed or unmanaged pooled virtual
  desktops to a secondary site.

- Replicate remote applications and sessions to a
  secondary site or Azure.

In the on-premises environment, we can have RDS deployed either on physical servers or as VMs running Hyper-V or VMware as a host platform. ASR can protect both on-premises and virtual deployments irrespective of the hypervisor platform (Hyper-V or VMware-based) used to the Azure site. Table 6-3 provides the different supported RDS deployments in site-to-Azure or site-to-site DR scenarios.

***Table 6-3.** RDS Deployments*

Deployment Type	Hyper-V Site-to-Site	Hyper-V Site-to-Azure	VMware Site-to-Azure	Physical Site-to-Azure
Pooled virtual desktop (unmanaged)	Yes	No	No	No
Pooled virtual desktop (managed, no User Profile Disks (UPD))	Yes	No	No	No
Remote Apps and desktop sessions (no UPD)	Yes	Yes	Yes	Yes

Prerequisites

Before configuring ASR for deployed RDS infrastructure, make sure to check that the following requirements are taken care of.

- Verify the on-premises RDS deployment and develop a clear understanding about the network and user access.

- Verify that the Azure Site Recovery Services Vault is created, and you have proper permission to configure and perform the replication and recovery.

- If you are going to use Azure as your recovery site, run the Azure Virtual Machine Readiness Assessment tool on your VMs to ensure they are compatible with Azure VMs and Azure Site Recovery Services.

Implementation Checklist

The following are the high-level implementation steps you should perform while planning and deploying protection for the RDS infrastructure on Azure using ASR.

1. Configure VMs for DR.

   - *Hyper-V:* Download the Microsoft Azure Site Recovery Provider. Install it on your VMM server or Hyper-V host. See the prerequisites for replication to Azure using ASR for information.

   - *VMware:* Configure the protection server, configuration server, and master target servers.

2. Prepare your resources.

   - Add an Azure Storage account.

   - *Hyper-V:* Download the Microsoft Azure Recovery Services Agent and install it on Hyper-V host servers.

   - *VMware:* Make sure the Mobility service is installed on all VMs.

   - Enable protection for VMs in the VMM cloud, Hyper-V sites, or VMware sites.

3. Design your recovery plan.

    • *Map your resources:* Map on-premises networks to Azure virtual networks.

    • Create the recovery plan.

    • Test the recovery plan by creating a test failover. Ensure all VMs can access required resources, like Active Directory. Ensure network redirections are configured and working for RDS.

4. Run a disaster recovery drill using planned and unplanned failovers. Ensure that all VMs have access to required resources, such as Active Directory and other dependent resources. For a better understanding of failovers and how to run drills depending on the scenario, whether it is Azure to Azure or on-premises to Azure, refer to Chapters 3 and 4.

RDS Disaster Recovery Using Azure Site Recovery

To be sure that our RDS environment is properly configured for DR, we should make sure that all the important components that make up your RDS run in an on-premises environment.

Configure Active Directory and DNS

If there is a small number of applications and a single DC for your entire on-premises site, and you will fail over the entire site together, use ASR-Replication to replicate the DC to the secondary site. On the other hand, if you have a large number of applications and are running an Active Directory forest, and you need to fail over only a few applications at a time, then in such case it is better to set up an additional DC on the DR site.

Set Up SQL Server Replication

Follow the procedure described in the earlier section "SQL High Availability and Disaster Recovery on Azure."

Enable Protection for RDS Components

As mentioned earlier, depending on the deployment model of RDS, we will take a different approach to protection. Configure the relevant ASR elements based on whether your VMs are deployed on Hyper-V or VMware.

- *Deployment type:* Personal virtual desktop (unmanaged)

  - Make sure all virtualization hosts are ready with the Remote Desktop Virtualization Host role installed.

  - Protect the Connection Broker.

  - Personal desktops.

  - Ensure Gold template VM.

  - Protect Web Access, License server, and Gateway server.

- *Deployment type:* Pooled virtual desktop (managed with no UPD)

  - Ensure all virtualization hosts are ready with the Remote Desktop Virtualization Host role installed.

  - Protect the Connection Broker.

  - Ensure Gold template VM.

  - Protect Web Access, License server, and Gateway server.

- *Deployment type:* RemoteApps and Desktop Sessions (no UPD)

  - Protect Session Hosts.

  - Protect the Connection Broker.

  - Protect Web Access, License server, and Gateway server.

Summary

In this chapter, we learned that specific applications should be treated differently, and standard tools for replication do not apply. As a best practice, always leverage the application-specific recovery solution or features to ensure data consistency and seamless recovery. We explored how the Active Directory infrastructure needs to be treated and what the available options are. We also looked at other critical workloads such as SQL Server, SAP, and RDS, and we learned about various approaches to design and build a recovery solution for them on Microsoft Azure. Each application is different in terms of functionality, technology stack, and underlying platform and architectural constructs. For example, an IIS-based web application and a line-of-business deep-sea exploration application are from two different worlds and should be treated differently. Not all applications will support ASR and Azure Backup. In fact, certain applications might not even have an availability construct. In all scenarios, though, there is always a certain degree of platform capabilities that we can leverage to ensure business continuity.

CHAPTER 7

Monitoring and Automation

Both monitoring and automation are crucial to a resilient system. Effective monitoring ensures timely detection and alerting of *what* failed, when it failed, and why. Automating various manual and prescriptive actions helps to reduce the amount of human error and minimize RTO. There are several factors that decide the degree and amount of monitoring and automation. Here are a few of them.

- *Type of application and its related components:* What you shouldmonitor and which parts you will be able to automate depend on the application type and its dependencies. For example, a web-based application hosted on-premises that depends on Windows Active Directory will require considerations for monitoring Active Directory access, health, and latency. If the application is an App Service developed and deployed on Azure, it will require at least endpoint monitoring if it is not dependent on Active Directory.

- *SLA requirements:* Lower SLA will require less automation and monitoring of some of the components, whereas higher SLA means more stringent monitoring and automation of every possible step.

© Bapi Chakraborty and Yashajeet Chowdhury 2020

B. Chakraborty and Y. Chowdhury, *Introducing Disaster Recovery with Microsoft Azure*,
https://doi.org/10.1007/978-1-4842-5917-7_7

- *Type of recovery in-place or planned:* Methods of automation and monitoring and how they will be achieved also depends on the type of recovery plan. For example, active-active DR scenarios are often more highly monitored and automated than the active-standby scenarios. Again, however, this depends on the application and the scenarios. In certain cases, if there are no redundant active deployments to handle a failure, the requirements to monitor for failure might be high.

- *Source and target location:* Source and target location also influence the monitoring and automation requirements. If both source and recovery locations are on-premises datacenters, using the same solution for automation will work. You also need to identify how and what will you monitor once the application has failed over. Similarly, if the source and target both are on the cloud, such as Microsoft Azure, the solutions that you might leverage will be cloud based, such as Azure Monitor, Azure Automation runbooks, and so on.

Every organization intends to use a single system that can provide end-to-end monitoring of applications hosted both on-premises and on Azure. Microsoft Azure provides a comprehensive monitoring platform and solution to monitor all infrastructure and platform resources. It helps by collecting, analyzing, monitoring, and reporting all logs and telemetry from various resources, making the process more operationally effective, efficient, secure, and proactive. In this chapter we explore Microsoft Azure monitoring and automation capabilities so that you can adopt solutions accordingly when it comes to Microsoft Azure.

Overview of Resource Monitoring with Microsoft Azure

DR is a process of restoring the functionality of an application in the event of a catastrophe. At times, a significant part of availability lies outside the application. Hence, detect and plan to monitor such components as well. The following are a few such cases.

- Dependent external services such as Active Directory, Human Resource Management System (HRMS), Customer Relationship Management (CRM), or any other data sources.

- Underlying network infrastructure.

- Build monitoring for each layer of the application such as data, business logic, integration, identity, and so on.

- Monitor for data corruption and recovery alerts.

Application and Resource Monitoring

Monitoring relevant resources of an application and the underlying platform helps you to detect a failure early and take the necessary actions. It helps to detect probable downtime based on an outage trend or detect a vulnerability of the system. For example, if one of the nodes of a two-node web server is unresponsive, it is a vulnerable system if the second node fails, too. Detecting the health and availability of important components of an application helps you make informed decisions.

Azure Monitor

Microsoft Azure Monitor is an end-to-end monitoring and diagnostic solution for both cloud and on-premises environments. It supports the entire life cycle of collecting, storing, analyzing, and reporting the data collected

261

from your VMs, containers, and other cloud-based resources such as virtual networks, Azure Storage, Application Gateway, and so on. You can use Azure monitoring data with Log Analytics for troubleshooting and diagnostic purposes. Act on the insights by creating alerts, sending an email, or logging a ticket into an incident management system such as Service Now. With Azure Monitor, you can collect, store, and analyze several elements.

- *Tenant monitoring logs:* These cover all operational aspects of your tenant or Azure Active Directory.

- *Subscription monitoring data:* This includes all activity-specific logs of your Azure subscription.

- *VM and container logs:* Connect and analyze logs from VMs and containers running on Azure, on-premises, or any other cloud.

- *Resource logs:* This is specific to various diagnostics and resource-specific logs on Azure; for example, Azure Storage, virtual network, NSGs, and so on.

- *Application logs:* With Application Insight, you can collect deep insights from your application code, performance, and functionality. It can be used to monitor applications developed in multiple platforms like .NET, Java, or Node.JS. It is also compatible with mobile apps. AppInsight enables easy integration with the Visual Studio App Center with installation of a small instrumentation package in your application. It sends telemetry information to the Application Insights service in Azure. Application Insights doesn't limit adding the instrumentation package to only applications hosted in Azure, which makes it a good choice for enterprises with large-scale hybrid cloud or multicloud deployments. The response time metrics collected by Application Insights help you keep tabs on the status of application availability. The resultant telemetry data can be accessed and analyzed using PowerBI, used for configuring alerts, integration into dashboards, and so on.

Traditionally, on-premises systems leverage various tools and solutions to monitor, collect logs, analyze, and report, such as System Center Operations Manager, Nagios, Zabbix, Riverbed, New Relic, Solar wind Scout, Splunk, and so on. However, with the advent of cloud technologies, there are new tools that help monitor applications with advanced insight and built in analytics. Similarly, for automation, newer concepts of resilient cloud-based architecture changed how various actions are automated.

Microsoft Azure produces extensive logging for every service. These logs are categorized into the following types.

- *Control/Management logs:* These logs give visibility into the Azure Resource Manager Create, Update, and Delete operations. These logs include Azure subscription-level and tenant-level events and operations, including any create, deploy, or delete resource operations or any Azure Active Directory level operational events.

- *Data Plane logs:* These give visibility into the events raised when using an Azure resource. Examples include Windows Event logs from an Azure VM, security and application logs in a VM, application-specific performance and functionality data, or any other Azure resource-specific data (e.g., NSG logs or Application Gateway diagnostic data).

We can enable these logs either by PowerShell, using the Azure Diagnostics Software Development Kit and Visual Studio, from the Azure Portal diagnostics and monitoring settings, or by using a JSON template incorporating the diagnostics extension. The resource-specific logs can be enabled either when we deploy the resource or at any time later.

You can also provide data to Azure Monitor from a custom resource using Data Collector APIs. This addresses any custom scenarios wherein the resources do not have an inherent way to provide any telemetry. More documentation can be found at `https://docs.microsoft.com/en-us/ azure/azure-monitor/platform/data-collector-api`.

Type of Data

Fundamentally there are two types of data in use in any monitoring system.

- *Logs:* Logs are sets of various data organized together to provide meaningful insights. They might contain additional properties or attributes. For example, Windows event logs consist of various kinds of data related to an event. They contain time, user, details of the event, an ID that references the event and is well documented, and so on. Other logs might be specific to a service, such as IIS logs, which contain service start, service stop, what is loaded, and what went wrong in the event of a failure of the service.

- *Metrics:* These provide point-in-time information or numerical values about system performance or other aspects of a service, such as CPU and memory usage collected in a specific interval over a period of time. Depending on requirements, we can choose the sampling interval, or calculate and interpret values

based on Max, Min, Avg, or Sum. Another interesting
example would be endpoints of an Azure Traffic
Manager or number of endpoints available at any point
in time for Azure Application Gateway.

Application Insight

Using Azure Monitor, at each resource level we are be able to collect
relevant data to identify issues and take appropriate actions. We will be
able to detect an endpoint failure, for example, and determine if a web
endpoint is accessible or not. Is the web service is functional? Is it able
to process data? Is it hung? Is the data being processed consistently?
Answers to these questions also form a part of the availability construct
of the application. The Azure platform is able to provide various matrices
and availability data points up to a certain extent, after which there has
to be another way to detect the absolute functionality monitoring of
the application. Many applications monitoring solutions today provide
capability for posting synthetic transactions to the web endpoint to be able
to identify if it really works. Along similar lines, Azure Application Insight
gives you deeper insights into the inner workings of your applications
and flags any performance or availability issues. This is faciliated by
deeper integration with the analytics platform that forms the core of Azure
Monitor. It can be used to monitor applications developed on multiple
platforms like .NET, Java, or Node.JS. It is also compatible with mobile
apps and can be used to monitor them by easy integration with the Visual
Studio App Center. You can also draw in telemetry information from the
host environments; for example, performance counters, diagnostics, or
docker logs. You can also set up web tests that periodically send synthetic
requests to your web service. Installation of a small instrumentation
package in your application is all it takes to send telemetry information
to the Application Insights service in Azure. Application Insights isn't
limited to applications hosted in Azure, which makes it a good choice for

enterprises with large-scale hybrid cloud or multicloud deployments. The response time metrics collected by Application Insights help you keep track of the status of application availability. The resultant telemetry data can be accessed and analyzed using PowerBi, used for configuring alerts, integrated into dashboards, and more. Figure 7-1 depicts high-level details of Application Insight data sources and visualization aspects.

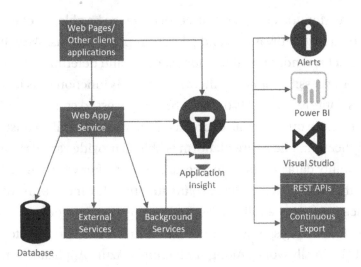

Figure 7-1. *Azure Application Insight*

Automation and Disaster Recovery

What should be automated for a recovery process is an interesting discussion point. There are various ways to look at automaton when it comes to DR. One thing that we need to be very careful about is triggering a DR process should be manual. If a trigger is automated, there is a possibility that the recovery process will be initiated due to a false positive, causing negative business impacts and possible outages. Hence, once a failure is logged, undertake an informed and manual intervention to decide if a recovery process must be invoked. Now let us look at automation in greater detail. Broadly, we can classify automation opportunities into the categories listed next.

- *Automated alerts:* Create various alerts for each maximum resource, failures, and exceptions. Automated alerts help to draw the attention of an operator to ensure action can be taken. Most monitoring systems have the capability to create alerts in the event a specific condition is met; for example, if a web endpoint is not available for more than five minutes in a specific region. Which specific thresholds, metrics, and events you need to create alerts for depends on the source application and infrastructure.

- *Trigger actions:* Create a support incident or send out an email or SMS based on the severity of the alert. This helps to determine the necessary action based on the severity of the issue. Some issues might be transient failures and that resolve with no intervention, in which case you might not want to create a support incident. However, you still want to monitor such an incident, and if the total count is more than ten in one hour, it will need some attention. Hence, the conditions and actions are important decision points for triggering a recovery process.

- *Automated failover:* The trigger to initiate a failover in the event of a disaster should not be automated. We can, however, automate various other aspects when recovering the workload. Recovering large, complex applications requires several steps, a set order, and stages in which certain tiers or modules need to recover. With Microsoft Azure recovery plans, you can invoke a runbook that can perform automated tasks. This requires an Automation account. This automated process to sequence, execute, and implement tasks is called orchestrated recovery. For example, an Automation runbook can be run to deploy an additional VM to deploy the application using a Continuous Integration/Continuous Deployment (CI/CD) process. Similarly, a postprovisioning script can join the system to a domain and add a data disk as part of the VM creation process in the recovery region. If the VM is already running, automation can validate the compute configuration and recover a specific tier of the application in a certain order. One should plan the entire orchestrated process of recovery around your application, its components, and its dependencies.

Monitoring Service Health and Azure Service Status

When using Azure services, the context of health monitoring includes the health of the Azure platform, health monitoring of specific Azure services, and a level deeper into the diagnostics of individual resources.

Azure Service Status Page

Azure provides a comprehensive status of the platform in multiple georgraphies on the service status page that can be accessed at `https://azure.microsoft.com/en-us/status/`. The current status as well as status history is available for review from that link. The status history shows previous outages, the root cause of the outage, mitigation, and next steps.

Azure Service Health Dashboard

The Service Health dashboard in Azure gives a personalized view of any Azure service outages as well as a summary of any potential impact to your resources. It can be used to create personalized dashboards and configured to send alerts, should there be an outage affecting your services.

It covers the following three types of events that could affect the health of deployed services:

- Ongoing service issues affecting your deployed Azure services.

- Scheduled platform maintenance activties that could affect service availability.

- Health advisories related to deprecated Azure services and features or notifications on exceeding the usage quota.

Azure Resource Health

- The health status of each resource can be seen by selecting the respective resource -> Support + Troubleshooting -> Resource Health. Any platform- or non-platform-related issues that could affect the availability of the service will be enumerated here. Additionally, workloads hosted in Azure VMs can have Azure Monitor for VMs enabled to give comprehensive component-level health data. This includes platform health, Guest VM health, and component health, as well as the health of core services like DHCP, DNS, Firewall, and so on (Figure 7-2).

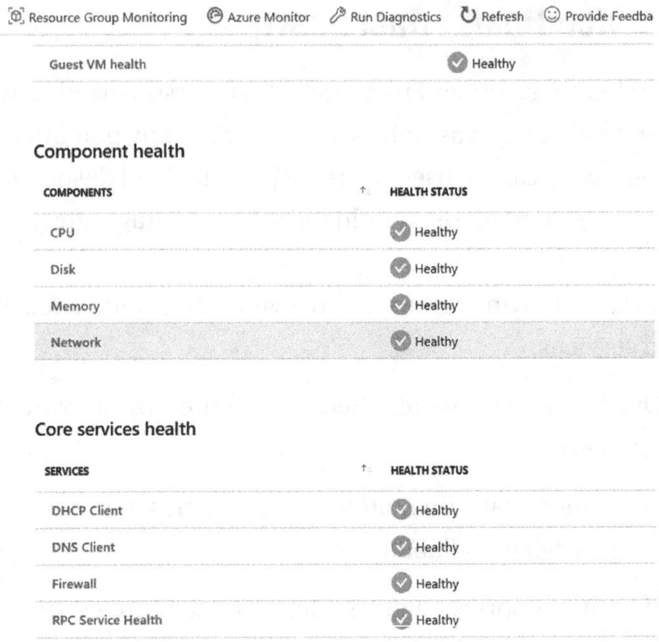

Figure 7-2. Azure resource sealth

Cost Management

Every solution comes with a price that needs to be kept to the minimum. Although, you can perform a cost–benefit analysis of various services and features, monitoring of the solution cost will help you procure or plan budgets. Just like any other investments in IT assets and software solutions, DR forms a part of it, too. There are several factors that might affect the cost of the solution. Three such significant items are mentioned here.

- *The type of the recovery solution:* An active-active solution will have a higher cost requirement than an active-passive solution. Also, the cost burden could be huge if there are dedicated resources for each application and no cost optimization was built in during the design phase.

- *The amount of time and the type of resources that will continue to run at the recovery site:* For example, if the recovery site runs an identical sized workload without any usage, it will eventually generate higher costs.

- *Number of DR drills and duration of time the recovery site will continue to run:* Although there will not be several times a year that any one performs DR drill or test failovers, yet this should be considered since it will add to the overall cost of recovery solution.

Microsoft Azure provides multiple ways to manage and monitor costs. The Azure Cost Management and Billing service helps you to identify service-wide cost breakdowns, actual cost, a forecast with current trends, and budget allocation. You can allocate budget at the Management Group level, Subscription level, or the Resource Group level. In addition to the default portal view, you can also create custom dashboards using PowerBI connectors. For advanced scenarios, you can use Azure Cost Management APIs to add cloud costs to your Azure applications.

Monitoring Azure Site Recovery

We all monitor applications and their dependencies for possible failures and exceptions. What about the recovery solution itself, though? What if the recovery solution is experiencing issues and no one knows about it? To avoid any surprises, it is important to monitor your recovery solution as well.

You might choose to use a marketplace solution or a specific vendor product such as DoubleTake or Veeam. Alternatively, you might choose to use ASR. It depends on your existing investments, the application, and its related components for the choice of the tool. The recovery solution could also be custom designed using Microsoft Azure Services such as ASR, Azure Backup, Storage accounts, Logic Apps, Traffic Manager, and so on, and include several Azure or on-premises based services. Creating a monitoring plan for the recovery solution is equally important. In this section we learn about monitoring ASR.

Monitor Using the Dashboard

Using the Azure Portal, you can monitor various aspects of ASR. You can then drill down further to find more information about the health of replication, details and status of the protected instances, backup job status, and more. The following sections cover some of the important items that we can monitor on ASR using the Azure Portal.

Backups and Site Recovery

The ASR Overview page provides high-level detail about the various services enabled and their status. For example, Figure 7-3 shows the number of backup items, any critical alerts for backup failures, number of jobs in progress, number of jobs that failed, and so on. It also shows any storage consumed by the service and type of storage. You can double-click each of these items to gather more details.

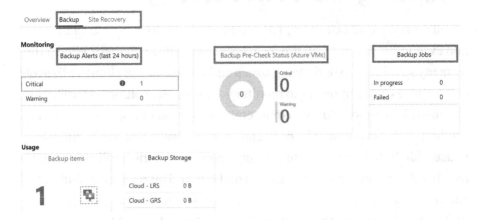

Figure 7-3. *ASR Overview page with backup summary*

Configuration Issues and Errors

Like backup, all Site Recoveryrelated details can be monitored from the portal as well. All Azure VMs and on-premises systems that are protected using ASR, their health state, configuration issues related to the process server, missing resource group or software updates, recovery plan, and so on, are depicted. It also shows the number of test failovers, success, and recommendations when no such test failover was done. Figure 7-4 represents the various items as they show up on the Azure Portal. In this case, we have limited details owing to only one VM that is protected.

Figure 7-4. *ASR Overview page with Site Recovery summary*

Infrastructure Monitoring

Infrastructure view provides high-level details of how various site recovery deployments look. It includes scenarios wherein the source workload is on Azure or on-premises (VMware, Hyper-V). You can also access a similar view but with very specific details from the VM VM002's resources menu operations and DR settings. It will be specific to that VM only, however. Figure 7-5 shows the Infrastructure view for an Azure-to-Azure replication for VM002. Any issues between the components will show up with a red line and a tool tip that describes the issue.

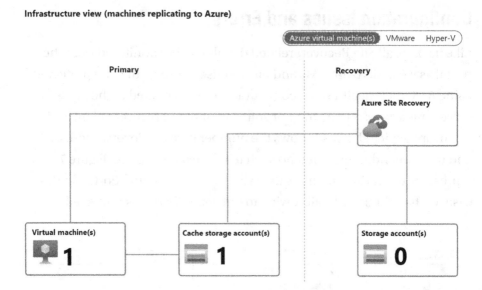

Figure 7-5. *ASR Overview page with Site Recovery Infrastructure view*

Figure 7-6 shows a VM-specific infrastructure view.

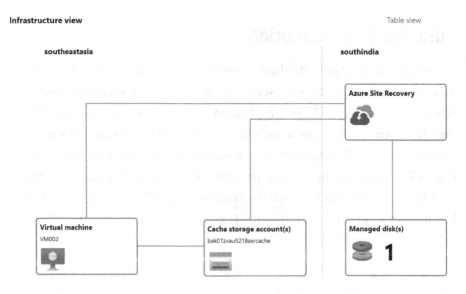

Figure 7-6. *Site Recovery Infrastructure view for VM002*

Note   As a best practice, ensure all protected instances and infrastructure components such as VMware machines, Hyper-V hosts, VMM hosts, process servers, and the configuration server are running the latest and updated agent or site recovery provider.

Test Failovers

To ensure all replicated items or application protection using ASR is working as expected, you should perform at least two failover tests in a year. A successful failover test includes successful cleanup of the entire environment postfailover as well. The Overview or summary page of Recovery Services Vaults shows all the previous successful, unsuccessful, and recommended test failover details. An architect of a recovery solution should include this consideration in the overall consumption cost for Azure services; that is, the cost involved in orchestrating an end-to-end DR scenario.

Recovery Plans

This shows the total number of recovery plans available. You can also create a new plan or update an existing one.

Jobs

Jobs summarizes all jobs executed within the last 24 hours. You can also view the status of jobs (completed, in progress, error). Drill down on each item to check further details on the job to identify an error, and so on. Alternatively, you can export the job details into an Excel file should you need to investigate any matter. Similarly, Backup jobs for site recovery provides details (e.g., operation type, backup or restore, time, status, duration and name of the resource, etc.) of all of the backup jobs run.

Alerts and Notifications

Responding to an unwanted event is important, so Azure provides various ways to stay informed when such an incident occur. The *Backup Alerts section* under Monitoring on the Azure Recovery Services Resource menu provides all the backup-related alerts and you can also *configure notifications.*

Site Recovery Events includes details such as server names, time, type of server (Azure VM or on-premises), and the severity of the events (critical, warnings, or informational). Event details include details such as replication health state change, recovery point creation for crash and application-consistent snapshots, power (on/off) state of the VM, and more.

Protected Items and Virtual Machines

The Replicated Items section of Recovery Services Vault provides details of all VMs that are protected: names, RPOs, location, health status, events, failover readiness, recovery points, and error details, if any. In the case of Azure Backup, the protected item lists all the various sources of the workloads that are configured; for example, Azure VMs, SAP VMs, SQL servers, registered System Center Data Protection Manager, Azure Backup Server, and Azure Backup agents that are installed in a server for files and folder backup. Figure 7-7 depicts a summary for all such protected items from various sources.

BACKUP MANAGEMENT TYPE	BACKUP ITEM COUNT
Azure Virtual Machine	1
SAP HANA in Azure VM	0
SQL in Azure VM	0
Azure Storage (Azure Files)	0
DPM	0
Azure Backup Server	0
Azure Backup Agent	0

Primary Region   *Secondary Region*

Figure 7-7. *Protected items in Azure Backup*

Process Server Health

When you deploy and configure DR of on-premises VMware or physical systems to Azure, a process server is deployed on-premises. Usually, a process server and configuration server are deployed together. However, depending on the load of the system (e.g., number of source VMs to be protected, their churn rate, network throughput across connected sources), multiple process servers will be deployed. Unhealthy process servers can negatively affect the RPO of the protected systems. Hence it is essential to monitor process servers. Here is how you can monitor a process server.

- Follow sizing and scaling guidance available on the Microsoft Azure documentation site at https:// docs.microsoft.com/en-us/azure/site-recovery/ site-recovery-plan-capacity-vmware#capacity- considerations for large-scale deployments. This helps to keep your monitoring proactive.

- Monitor process server health using the Azure Portal.
  You can access the VM that you wish to monitor from
  Replicated items in the Recovery Services Vault. Check
  the overall health status of the VM and the process
  server health associated with it. You can drill down
  further to identify the various alerts related to CPU,
  memory, free space, and so on. If the process server
  is deployed along with the configuration server, the
  configuration state of the same system is displayed
  as well. You can also access the health state of all the
  process severs registered to a configuration server. The
  Azure Recovery Services Infrastructure Configuration
  section in the Resource menu lists all the configuration
  servers and the associated process servers. You can
  drill down further to check the health of each process
  server.

Monitor Using Azure Monitor

As we discussed earlier, each Azure resource generates logs and diagnostic
data. ASR is no different. You can monitor various activity logs and
diagnostic logs using Azure Monitor. Once we configure Azure Monitor
to collect all relevant logs and diagnostics information from ASR, we can
analyze them interactively using Log Analytics and identify various issues.
You can monitor server health, recovery events, failover status, job status,
and more. You can also create alerts based on the log data. Azure Monitor
logs support Azure-to-Azure and VMware/physical system to Azure
replication scenarios.

To achieve this, you need some basic knowledge of writing Log
Analytics queries, a Log Analytics workspace, and the rights to relevant
protected instances. To understand the relevant settings let's look at
Figure 7-8.

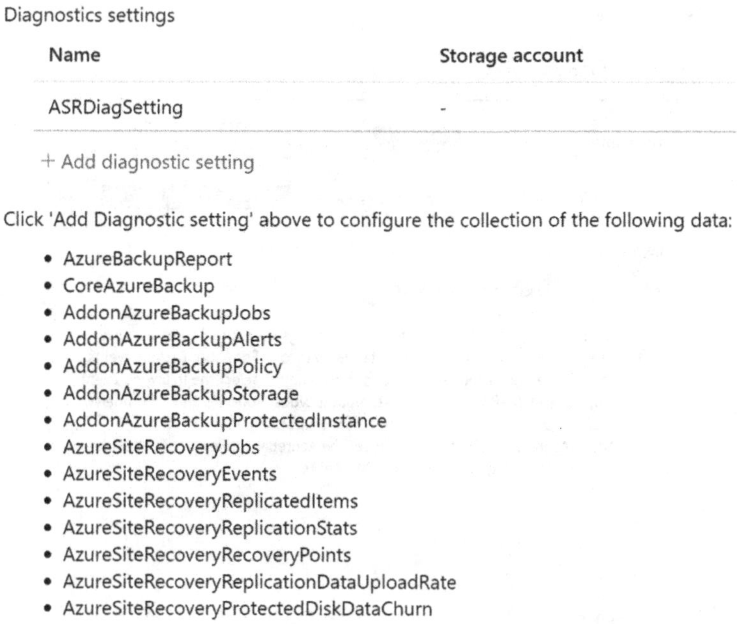

Diagnostics settings

Name	Storage account
ASRDiagSetting	-

+ Add diagnostic setting

Click 'Add Diagnostic setting' above to configure the collection of the following data:

- AzureBackupReport
- CoreAzureBackup
- AddonAzureBackupJobs
- AddonAzureBackupAlerts
- AddonAzureBackupPolicy
- AddonAzureBackupStorage
- AddonAzureBackupProtectedInstance
- AzureSiteRecoveryJobs
- AzureSiteRecoveryEvents
- AzureSiteRecoveryReplicatedItems
- AzureSiteRecoveryReplicationStats
- AzureSiteRecoveryRecoveryPoints
- AzureSiteRecoveryReplicationDataUploadRate
- AzureSiteRecoveryProtectedDiskDataChurn

Figure 7-8. *Logs and Diagnostics data for Recovery Services*

1. Access the Diagnostics Settings from the Resources menu of Recovery Services Vault.

2. Select the relevant logs for Backup and site recovery from the given list and choose either Log Analytics, Storage account for long-term retention or Event Hub for further integration as the destination. It is recommended that you create two different settings for Azure Backup and Site Secovery as detailed in Figure 7-9.

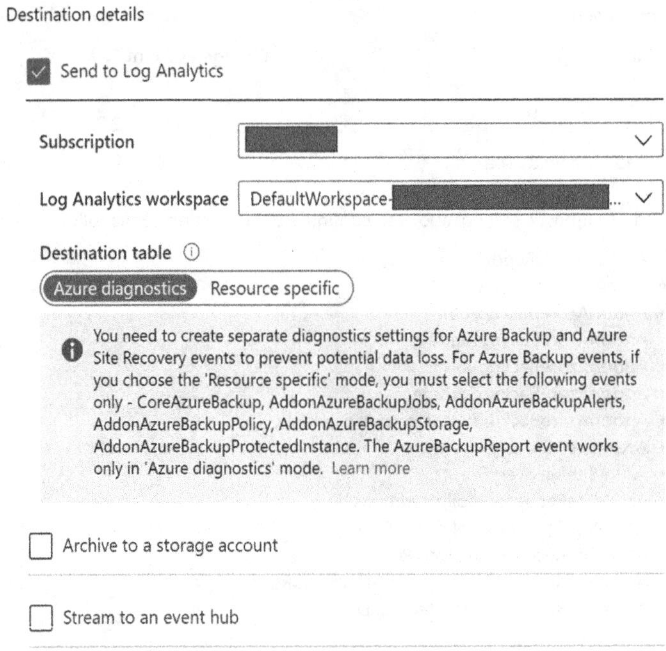

Destination details

☑ Send to Log Analytics

Subscription ▢

Log Analytics workspace DefaultWorkspace-▮ ... ∨

Destination table ⓘ

(**Azure diagnostics**   Resource specific)

> ⓘ You need to create separate diagnostics settings for Azure Backup and Azure Site Recovery events to prevent potential data loss. For Azure Backup events, if you choose the 'Resource specific' mode, you must select the following events only - CoreAzureBackup, AddonAzureBackupJobs, AddonAzureBackupAlerts, AddonAzureBackupPolicy, AddonAzureBackupStorage, AddonAzureBackupProtectedInstance. The AzureBackupReport event works only in 'Azure diagnostics' mode. Learn more

☐ Archive to a storage account

☐ Stream to an event hub

Figure 7-9. *Protected items in Azure Backup*

3. To include additional details on churn rate and throughput rate from process servers, you need download the Log Analytics agent manually, install it on the process server, and add the following two performance counters into the data page of data collection settings.

```
ASRAnalytics(*)\SourceVmChurnRate
ASRAnalytics(*)\SourceVmThrpRate
```

Once data is in Log Analytics, you can query interactively to generate various reports. The following query in Log Analytics generates a pie chart for total count of VMs that has RTO between 15 and 30 minutes and more than 30 minutes.

```
AzureDiagnostics
| where replicationProviderName_s == "A2A"
| where isnotempty(name_s) and isnotnull(name_s)
| extend RPO = case(rpoInSeconds_d <= 1800, "15-30Min", ">30Min")
| summarize hint.strategy=partitioned arg_max(TimeGenerated, *)
  by name_s
| project name_s , RPO
| summarize Count = count() by RPO
| render piechart
```

Example output is displayed in the output pane shown in Figure 7-10.

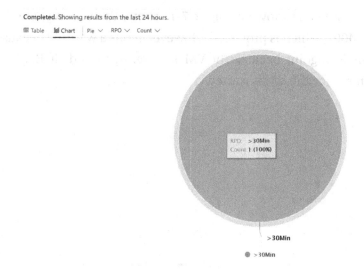

Figure 7-10. RTO result of Log Analytics query result

This second example generates a report of all the Azure VMs protected in another Azure region.

```
AzureDiagnostics
| where replicationProviderName_s == "A2A"
| where isnotempty(name_s) and isnotnull(name_s)
| summarize hint.strategy=partitioned arg_max(TimeGenerated, *)
  by name_s
| project VirtualMachine = name_s , Vault = Resource ,
  ReplicationHealth = replicationHealth_s, Status =
  protectionState_s, RPO_in_seconds = rpoInSeconds_d,
  TestFailoverStatus = failoverHealth_s, AgentVersion =
  agentVersion_s, ReplicationError = replicationHealthErrors_s,
  SourceLocation = primaryFabricName_s
```

The output table shown in Figure 7-11 shows there is only one VM named VM002, which is protected. However, it has a warning because no replication is ongoing because the VM is currently turned off. Replication will resume once the VM is started.

VirtualMachine	Vault	ReplicationHealth	Status	RPO_in_seconds	TestFailoverStatus	AgentVersior
VM002	VAULT218	Warning	Protected	14,035	Normal	9.32.5487.1

VirtualMachine	VM002
Vault	VAULT218
ReplicationHealth	Warning
Status	Protected
RPO_in_seconds	14035
TestFailoverStatus	Normal
AgentVersion	9.32.5487.1
> ReplicationError	[{ "errorCategory": "Replication", "possibleCauses": "The virtual machine is powered off and is not replicating currently.", "
SourceLocation	Southeast Asia

Figure 7-11. *Summary table of Azure VMs replicated to the secondary region*

The following example query depicts RPO of a VM named VM002 for the last five hours. Figure 7-12 renders the details in tabular format. We see that the RPO has increased tremendously. In this case the system VM002 was shut down and the replication paused, causing the RPO to rise.

```
AzureDiagnostics
| where replicationProviderName_s == "A2A"
| where TimeGenerated > ago(10h)
| where isnotempty(name_s) and isnotnull(name_s)
| where name_s == "VM002"
| project TimeGenerated, name_s , RPO_in_seconds = rpoInSeconds_d
```

TimeGenerated [UTC]	name_s	RPO_in_seconds
> 3/11/2020, 8:23:55.995 AM	VM002	10,996
> 3/11/2020, 8:10:56.041 AM	VM002	10,240
> 3/11/2020, 8:35:50.469 AM	VM002	11,735
> 3/11/2020, 7:58:05.567 AM	VM002	9,444
> 3/11/2020, 8:49:35.339 AM	VM002	12,560
> 3/11/2020, 4:34:39.792 AM	VM002	265
> 3/11/2020, 4:10:50.400 AM	VM002	302
> 3/11/2020, 4:15:51.585 AM	VM002	41
> 3/11/2020, 4:20:56.960 AM	VM002	46
> 3/11/2020, 4:22:16.681 AM	VM002	121
> 3/11/2020, 4:30:31.506 AM	VM002	20
> 3/11/2020, 5:38:25.298 AM	VM002	1,087
> 3/11/2020, 4:05:48.530 AM	VM002	38

Figure 7-12. *RPO result of Log Analytics query for VM002*

Now that we have logged all that good information into Azure Monitor logs and we know how to derive results from Log Analytics that matter to your business, you can take actions based on them. Create the necessary log alerts based on the query output condition right out of the Log Analytics portal. Figure 7-13 shows the command bar from which you can create an alert to send out an email, send an SMS, raise an incident, and so on. You can also choose send a JSON payload to be executed that can perform other actions such as trigger Log Apps to drop a message to an Azure Queue, send a Slack message, or run an Azure Automation runbook.

```
New Query 1*      New Query...*×   +
ultWorkspace-4474b8ee... Select Scope   ▷ Run    Time range : Last 24 hours   🖫 Save   ℗ Copy link ∨   + New alert rule   ↦ Export ∨
AzureDiagnostics
| where replicationProviderName_s == "A2A"
| where isnotempty(name_s) and isnotnull(name_s)
| summarize hint.strategy=partitioned arg_max(TimeGenerated, *) by name_s
| project VirtualMachine = name_s , Vault = Resource , ReplicationHealth = replicationHealth_s, Status = protectionState_s,
```

Figure 7-13. *Create a new log alert based on Log Analytics results*

Summary

In this chapter, we looked at how monitoring and automation are important to your overall recovery plans. Each resource on Azure generates various logs and diagnostic data that can be collected and stored in various ways. Monitoring helps to identify a problem, and then log, analyze, and raise an alert so that appropriate action can be taken. The action can be manual or automated. You can use Azure Monitor, Application Insight, Log Analytics, Query language, and built-in Action groups to create an end-to-end solution. With regard to automation, automate what is necessary, but avoid automating everything to avoid false positives. We primarily discussed Azure services and various constructs. A similar solution outline can be achieved on-premises as well. A simple example could be using System Center Operations Manager to monitor and identify issues and Integrated System Center Orchestrator to create and trigger various PowerShell workflows to perform the necessary automated actions to log events and take action on them. Azure services take you to the next level of automation and recovery capabilities so that you can achieve your SLA and business goals effectively and efficiently.

CHAPTER 8

Final Words and Exercises

Every organization is different. For each one, the workload is varied based on how old it is, what industry is belongs to, its level of technical adoption, the type of customer data it handles, and length and breadth of its application portfolio. Depending on what DR means for each such type of organization, its unique application portfolio decides the solution it wants to adopt. Remember a disaster recovery solution is more than a technology product; it is a solution that is heavily process dependent. There should be adequate documentation and definition of what, how, who, and when to be able to recover a workload. In addition to coordination among various groups, the end-to-end process should be outlined and baked in as part of the DR solution. Most important, measure your confidence level on the solution. Will it work when you need it the most? Have you tested it enough end to end? Did all the parts come together well? Did everyone do what they needed to do? Are you detecting all the failures and exceptions? When do you trigger a DR? When do you take the call to do that seriously? Did your target environment recover during the planned RTO? Was application consistency achieved with the desired RPO? Challenges will be varied because this is a process and not the execution of technology.

© Bapi Chakraborty and Yashajeet Chowdhury 2020
B. Chakraborty and Y. Chowdhury, *Introducing Disaster Recovery with Microsoft Azure*,
https://doi.org/10.1007/978-1-4842-5917-7_8

A Few Final Words

By now, you have learned about and explored various DR constructs, the capabilities of Microsoft Azure, and considerations required to design an efficient, cost-effective solution. The chapters in this book are designed to provide you with a ground-up view on DR, Microsoft Azure, its services, tools, and capabilities. Whether you are a consultant, a solution architect considering Microsoft Azure for the first time, or an administrator already hosting some of your workloads on Azure and considering its tools and capabilities to design a DR solution, we took you on a journey to provide a 360-degree view. Certainly this is not everything, and there is much more to explore. When you look at modern architectures, industry-specific applications, or composite solutions and start developing a DR solution, that is when the entire blurry image starts to come together. For a clearer picture, each section of the source application, its infrastructure, organization processes, tools, and technology need to be ironed out. Think about a blockchain workflow application, advanced workloads like SAP or other Enterprise Resource Planning (ERP) stacks, and the efforts, process, and technology required to create a recovery solution. Along similar lines, advanced analytics and industry scaled solutions like financial fraud detection, deep-sea exploration, and so on, will require very different considerations.

Microsoft Cloud is an ever-evolving platform; features and capabilities are introduced by the thousands every year. This paves a path for the unlimited possibilities and scenarios that we can achieve. With added focus to support more and more partner solutions, open source products make Microsoft Azure a preferred destination to host your workloads. The end-to-end hybrid cloud architecture with Azure stack and Azure support for identity, network, security, manageability, and storage enables hybrid deployment, seamless integration, and portability. It is a complete trusted platform.

We conclude this book with this chapter, but we intend to leave you with a few scenarios that you can use to design a recovery solution. Once you create and chalk out these DR solutions, look at the Azure Architecture Center on Microsoft Azure documentation center for some of the application and solution patterns. Use these application patterns and try to create a DR solution with all possible combinations such as active-active, active-passive with warm, and active-passive with cold patterns. Then, create a sample application, deploy it, and test it. Run DR drills and build confidence in what you have created. There is no better way to know whether your solution will work than thorough testing.

Exercises

Here we provide a few scenarios that give a sample deployment of an imaginary application. Try to apply all the discovery, planning, design constructs, tools, methodologies, technology, and platform capabilities we have discussed so far and create an end-to-end recovery and failback solution for each of them. We have included a small *"Hint"* section for your reference. We encourage you to perform your own research in addition to applying the details included in this book and identify a robust recovery solution coupled with monitoring, management, and automation.

Exercise 1

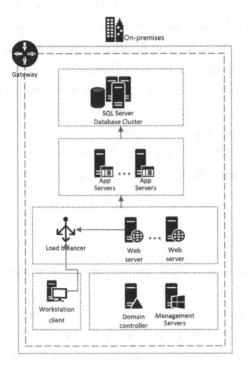

Figure 8-1. *On-premises deployment of a multitier web application*

Scenario: Figure 8-1 shows a three-tier web application hosted on-premises. It does not depend on any directory services for authentication and authorization. The application has its own authentication mechanism. Each tier of the application as shown in Figure 8-1 (web, app, and data) is hosted by a set of two physical servers. The web tier is load balanced by a network load balancer. The application tier and data tier are hosted in a Microsoft Windows-based cluster. The web servers are Windows 2012 R2 IIS servers and the database is SQL Server 2012 on Windows 2012 R2 and uses SQL Server AlwaysOn AG.

Requirement: The enterprise understands that it is a critical application and implements only backup and restore as their recovery strategy. They have recently adopted Microsoft Azure and would like to use available cloud-based recovery services with Azure as a target location. You are assigned the task of designing and implementing the DR solution for this application. Key requirements are minimal downtime during recovery drills, testing capability, and ensuring end-to-end recovery with minimal human intervention. You are required to produce the following elements before implementing the solution.

- Available alternative options for each tier for recovery.

- A plan for each tier-level failure, instance-level failure, and entire solution failure.

- A high-level solution architecture document detailing how the end-to-end recovery solution will work.

- A detailed low-level implementation and configuration document for the failover and failback plan.

- Include monitoring, management, and automation aspects that will help effective identification and timely action.

Hint

ASR	Helps to create a recovery solution on Azure for physical on-premises workloads. Review Chapters 2 and 4 for details.
SQL servers	Check Chapter 6 for application-specific workload DR options. Check if managed SQL databases could be leveraged.
Load balancer	Azure internal/external load balancer
Network	Site-to-site or ExpressRoute
Backup	Review Azure Backup with Recovery Services Vault and SQL application backups.

Exercise 2

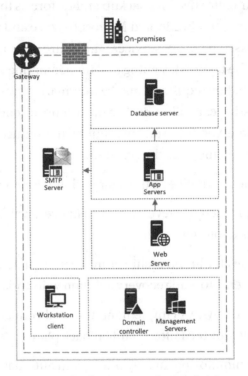

Figure 8-2. *On-premises deployment of a multitier web application with SMTP integration*

Scenario: Figure 8-2 is a three-tier web application hosted on-premises. It depends on Windows Active Directory services for authentication and authorization. Each tier of the application as shown in Figure 8-2 (web, app, and data) is hosted by a single highly available VM hosted in a Hyper-V host cluster managed by SCVMM. The web server is a Windows 2008 R2 IIS server and the database is an Oracle server. The application uses SMTP server on-premises to send emails as well and there are no plans to migrate the SMTP server anywhere.

   Requirement: The enterprise understands that it is a critical application and implements backup and restore as their only recovery strategy. They have recently adopted Microsoft Azure and would like to use available cloud-based recovery services with Azure as a target location. You are assigned to design and implement the DR solution for this application. Key considerations are minimal downtime during recovery drills, testing capability, and ensuring end-to-end recovery with minimal human intervention. Also, the enterprise wants to ensure that the solution is highly available and resilient against any single datacenter failure. You are required to produce the following elements before implementing the solution.

- Available alternative options for each tier for recovery with the supportability matrix in mind. Set down your assumptions of the solution as applicable.

- Plan for each tier-level failure, instance-level failure, and entire solution failure.

- A high-level solution architecture document detailing how the end-to-end recovery solution will work.

- A detailed low-level implementation and configuration document for the failover and failback plan.

- Include monitoring, management, and automation aspects that will help effective identification and timely action.

Hint

ASR	Helps to create a recovery solution on Azure for physical on-premises workloads. Review Chapters 2 and 4 for details.
Network	Site-to-site or ExpressRoute. Review Chapter 3. Also research additional details on ExpressRoute with multiple regional connections and routing and how it helps in designing DR scenarios that involve multiple regions or datacenters.
Backup	Review Azure Backup with Recovery Services Vault.
On-premises integration	Additional routing needs to be taken care for SMTP integration including Firewall and NSG configurations.

Exercise 3

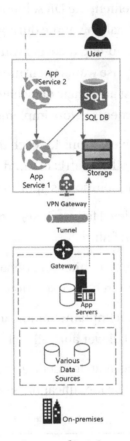

Figure 8-3. *Azure app service application with on-premises integration*

Scenario: Figure 8-3 is a simple web application hosted on Azure and is externally accessible. The enterprise wishes to enhance the security of the application by ensuring that the application is protected against web-based attacks. There are two web apps that use one SQL database and a storage account. The application is dependent on the data that is processed by an on-premises application server.

The application server connects to various internal on-premises data sources and applications, massages the data, and connects to an Azure Storage account to store the transformed data in a specific container. The Web App 1 on Azure runs a web job on a schedule, picks up the new data, performs further changes, and stores the data into another container in the same Storage account and also a reference in the SQL database. The Web App 2 on Azure that is accessed by various users uses the SQL database and the Storage account to serve the data stored in them.

Requirement: The enterprise understands that it is a critical application and implements backup and restore as their only recovery strategy. They have recently adopted Microsoft Azure and would like to use available cloud-based recovery services with Azure as a target location. You are assigned the task of designing and implementing the DR solution for this application. Important requirements are minimal possible downtime during recovery drills, testing capability, and ensuring end-to-end recovery with minimal human intervention. Also, as described in the scenario, make necessary inclusions to enhance the security posture of the solution. You are required to produce the following elements before implementing the solution.

- Available alternative options for each tier for security and recovery with the supportability matrix in mind. Outline your assumptions of the solution as applicable.

- Plan for each tier or level of failure, including instance-level failure and entire solution failure.

- A high-level solution architecture document detailing how the end-to-end recovery solution will work.

- A detailed low-level implementation and configuration document for the failover and failback plan.

- Include monitoring, management, and automation aspects that will help effective identification and timely action.

Hint

Azure App Services	Managed services protection and recovery. Review Chapter 3.
Network	Site-to-site or ExpressRoute; Research additional details on ExpressRoute with multiple region connections and routing and how it helps with designing DR scenarios that involve multiple regions or datacenters.
Backup	Review Azure Backup with Recovery Services Vault.
SQL Database	SQL database geo-replication; backup and recovery, Chapters 3 and 6.
Azure Storage account	GRS or RA-GRS storage account; Chapter 3.

Exercise 4

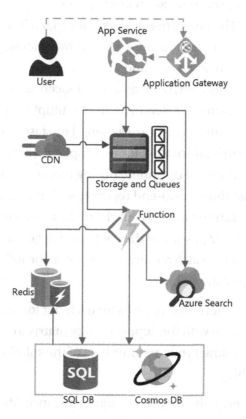

Figure 8-4. *Azure App service application with on-premises integration*

Scenario: Figure 8-4 is a web application hosted on Azure and externally accessible via an application gateway configured in WAF mode. Users upload their files using the web interface. The Web App Service uses a queue and storage account to store the file. It also uses a SQL database and Cosmos DB for storing configuration details, users' details, and various metadata. Based on a file upload event, a function app performs further processing of the file. Both the function app and Web app use Redis for caching and Azure Search indexing. For static data delivery to users, Azure CDN uses the Storage account as an origin point.

Requirement: The enterprise understands that it is a critical application. However, currently there is no recovery strategy. They have recently adopted Microsoft Azure and would like to use available cloud-based recovery services with Azure as a target location as well. They would also like to expand this deployment to multiple regions and serve users from various countries. You are assigned the task of designing and implementing the DR solution for this application. Important considerations are minimal downtime during recovery drills, testing capability, and ensuring end-to-end recovery with minimal human intervention. As described in the scenario, make the necessary inclusions to enhance the security posture of the solution. Suggest both hot DR and cold DR options. You are also required to produce the following elements before implementing the solution.

- Available alternative options for each tier for security and recovery with the supportability matrix in mind. Set down your assumptions of the solution as applicable.

- Plan for each tier or level of failure, instance-level failure and entire solution failure.

- A high-level solution architecture document detailing how the end-to-end recovery solution will work.

- A detailed low-level implementation and configuration document for the failover and failback plan.

- Include monitoring, management, and automation aspects that will help effective identification and timely action.

Hint

- Review Chapters 3 and 6 and Azure online
  documentation of relevant services for creating the
  recovery solution blueprint and then expand on it.

Exercise 5

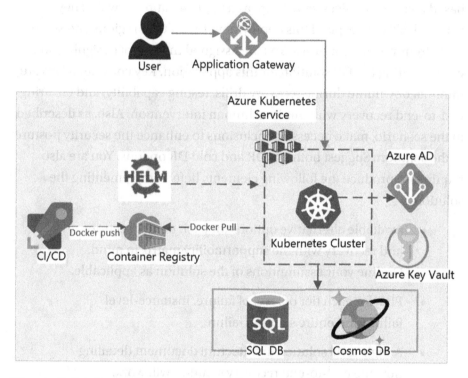

Figure 8-5. *Azure App service application with on-premises integration*

Scenario: The organization you are working for is developing all their new applications based on microservices and dockers. They have a multitenant application deployed in a Kubernetes-based cluster on Azure and accessible over the Internet. It uses an SQL database and Cosmos DB for its storage. Azure Active Directory is used for identity and authentication and the Azure Key Vault securely stores and accesses all secrets, keys, database strings, and so on. The Azure pipeline is used for CI/CD of the services. All container images are published into the Container Registry.

Requirement: The enterprise understands that it is a critical application. However, currently there is no recovery strategy. They have recently adopted Microsoft Azure and would like to use available cloud-based recovery services with Azure as a target location as well. They would also like to expand this deployment to multiple regions and serve users from various countries. You are assigned the task of designing and implementing the DR solution for this application. Key considerations are minimal downtime during recovery drills, testing capability, and ensuring end-to-end recovery with minimal human intervention. Also, as described in the scenario, make necessary inclusions to enhance the security posture of the solution. Suggest both hot DR and cold DR options. You are also required to produce the following elements before implementing the solution.

- Available alternative options for each tier for security and recovery with the supportability matrix in mind. Outline your assumptions of the solution as applicable.

- Plan for each tier or level of failure, instance-level failure and entire solution failure.

- A high-level solution architecture document detailing how the end-to-end recovery solution will work.

- A detailed low-level implementation and configuration document for the failover and failback plan.

- Include monitoring, management, and automation aspects that will help effective identification and timely action.

Hint

- Review Chapters 3 and 6 and the Azure online documentation of relevant services for creating the recovery solution blueprint and then expand on it.

- Additional discovery and consideration requirements for the AKS cluster per `https://docs.microsoft.com/en-us/azure/aks/concepts-network`.

Index

A

Active-active disaster recovery
method, 28, 33
Advanced Business Application
Programming (ABAP)
application servers, 243
Advanced network
management, 48
Agile methodologies, 32
AlwaysOn Availability Group,
232–234
AlwaysOn Failover Cluster
instance, 231, 232
Amazon Web Services (AWS), 32
API Management service, 131, 136
Application backup considerations,
130–132
Application-level replication
technologies, 40
Applications
configuration, 208
connectivity, 208
design architectures, 34
enterprise, 35
gateway, 131
IaaS and PaaS services
recovery solution, 121–125

scenario, 120, 121
industrialized, 35
legacy n-tier, 34
logs, 262
modern, 34
patterns and practices, 34
rehosted/refactored, 35
special workloads, 35
ASR Deployment Planner tool,
149–151, 160
Assumed failure, 23–25
Automated alerts, 267
Automated failover, 267
Automatic resource creation, 82
Automation, 31
automated alerts, 267
factors, 259, 260
failover, 267
scripts, 96
trigger actions, 267
Availability set, 38
Availability zone, 38
Azure Active Directory, 130, 298
Azure API Management service,
112, 126
Azure application gateway, 113
Azure application insight, 265, 266

© Bapi Chakraborty and Yashajeet Chowdhury 2020
B. Chakraborty and Y. Chowdhury, *Introducing Disaster Recovery with Microsoft Azure*,
https://doi.org/10.1007/978-1-4842-5917-7

Printed in the United States
By Bookmasters